No-Cook Meals

for Your

Food Storage

Add Nutrition and Variety

to Your Pantry

Millie Copper

Disclaimer

I am not a healthcare professional. I am a mom who believes that we are on the correct path for providing nutrient-dense, nourishing foods. You should do your own research and come to your own conclusions for your healthcare and nutrition, along with consulting a healthcare professional. I highly recommend contacting the Chapter Leader of your local Weston A. Price Foundation to ask about a list of healthcare providers.

Table of Contents

Introduction

Since 2009, I've made my home in Wyoming. One of the things Wyoming is known for is its long, cold winters. There are often high winds and blizzard-like conditions. Most of us understand that when a big storm comes, we may be stuck for days. Living rurally, with the nearest grocery store a 40-minute drive in perfect weather, we take our preparation for the season seriously. It's highly likely a weather event will leave us homebound.

Also, within the realm of normal, the electricity will flicker on and off, possibly finally giving up, and it'll be out until a line crew can do the necessary repairs. While our electricity provider does a great job of getting us back online, even in the middle of a blizzard, it could be several hours or stretch to several days. Winter weather is a reason we prep—because an incoming snowstorm, or other natural disaster, is a real possibility.

You may live in a less harsh winter climate without the threat of blizzards. Before moving to Wyoming, I lived in the Pacific Northwest for 20 years. Compared to Wyoming, the weather there is considerably mild. But it was a PNW weather event—not a Wyoming blizzard—that brought me to the preparedness world.

The Great Coastal Gale of 2007 produced two days of hurricane-force winds and heavy rains. Our power was knocked out on a Sunday, and we didn't get it back until Saturday. Others in the county were without electricity even longer. The winds blew so hard and did so much damage, large trees were ripped up by their roots. Windows in town were blown out, leaving a disaster in its wake. Gas stations were closed.

The bank was open—sort of. We could ring the bell at the back door, and they'd allow us $100 in cash with proof we had an account. Without electricity, there was no way to access the accounts (or ATMs), so it was a good-will gesture on the part of the bank.

The grocery store on the east side of town was cash only, with limited items available. What was available had been moved to the front of the store, and the rest of the building was cordoned off. The other grocery stores in the area remained closed. After a day or two, one or two fuel stations set up generators to operate. There was a two-gallon limit, and the lines snaked into the roads.

There were deaths and unbelievable damage.

After the worst of the storm passed, the cleanup began. More than one business never fully operated again. A candy store couldn't salvage their machinery after it was covered in glass, and they decided it was easier just to close the business.

When the electricity returned, things were still not normal. The stores and gas stations couldn't operate fully until supply trucks came to restock. The storm produced lots of flooding in nearby areas, making travel difficult.

Then it came to a screeching halt when the state highway into our rural coastal town had a major landslide. A massive 300-foot-long wall of mud, trees, and rocks was up to six feet deep in places. The road was closed for weeks, and all traffic was required to take a much longer detour, also on storm damaged roads.

Your threat may be severe rains or floods, hurricanes, tornadoes, earthquakes, wildfires, or a whole host of other weather-related or even man-made threats. Some of these situations, such as a hurricane, may require evacuation. For other situations, you're often hunkering down at home. We all got a crash course in staying home during the early months of the pandemic. While grocery stores were open in most areas, access was limited, as was availability.

The lockdowns of the pandemic were a wake-up call for many, especially when they went to the store and their favorite item(s) were unavailable due to shortages of both goods and employees throughout the supply chain.

With restaurants closed or limited, many people were forced to rely on home-cooked meals made with whatever was available in the store. My local grocers were short on basic items like pasta, sauces, easy-to-cook meats, and—of course—toilet paper. Fortunately, our previous planning left us comfortable during the lockdown and able to aid others.

Preparedness and food storage isn't just relegated to storms or worldwide pandemic scenarios. Preparation for things like unemployment and illness is smart. Imagine how wonderful it'd be to know you have a pantry full of food if you suddenly found yourself out of work!

I have a friend who experienced just that. Her husband lost his job during the Great Recession of 2007 to 2009. He was unemployed or underemployed for over a year. They relied on their food storage items for their meals, rarely able to supplement with newly purchased goods.

A website I enjoy, The Prudent Homemaker, shared a similar story of eating from their food storage during a time of economic downturn. Yet another person I know online shared how their food storage kept them fed during their son's illness and subsequent death. Not needing to go shopping was a relief for her during that terrible time.

Having a well-stocked pantry is important to my family. Also important is eating a healthy and nourishing diet. Around the same time we began our preparedness efforts, we learned about traditional foods and the work of Weston A. Price.

Dr. Price was a dentist who, in the 1930s and '40s, traveled the world to investigate the correlation between diet and dental health. He concentrated his efforts on communities that were traditional and isolated, untouched by modern foods. He found the isolated people not only had excellent dental health, but also physical and mental health. This was in contrast to what he was seeing in the industrialized areas with their processed and convenience foods.

Even in the '30s and '40s, there were plenty of processed oils, white flour, and sugary treats. Dr. Price believed there was a correlation between these foods and deteriorating health. His book *Nutrition and Physical Degeneration* details his findings.

The Weston A. Price Foundation, founded in 1999 by Sally Fallon and Mary G. Enig, promotes and continues Dr. Price's teachings. The women also authored the book *Nourishing Traditions*. The Foundation, commonly referred to as WAPF, has worldwide chapters disseminating Dr. Price's teachings and *Nourishing Traditions*.

The *Nourishing Traditions* book contains nearly 700 pages of information on traditional diets and recipes. I'll admit, the book is overwhelming. When I first got it, my eyes glazed over as I tried to comprehend the mass amount of information. I'll also admit, I saw dollar signs on every page. I was convinced there was no way an average family like mine could ever eat the foods being promoted in the book. Organic produce, grass-fed beef, supplements galore . . . it was all out of reach.

A few weeks later, after a severe gut ache, I knew something had to change. One of the reasons I'd started researching traditional foods was the rumor it would help with stomach problems. I'd been diagnosed with irritable bowel syndrome several years earlier. My husband also suffered from similar issues, and my youngest daughter was developing the same troubles.

As I broke down the book, I began to see places where we—on our modest income—could make some changes. Our Wyoming location didn't offer much in the way of organic food, especially in the winter, but we did discover a resource for grass-fed beef that offered a monthly CSA (Community Supported Agriculture), which would give us a small amount of meat at a price we could afford.

And since we were stocking up on beans already, we just switched to cooking them in the traditional way (long soaks followed by a long, slow cook or a long soak and then sprouting and cooking). That year, new to Wyoming and not yet residents, we were also able to purchase an inexpensive doe antelope tag for a little extra meat.

The first year we were in Wyoming, which was the first year we were serious about both preparedness and traditional foods, we ate more beans than I'd ever thought possible! I'd started a blog (called Real Food For Less Money at that time) detailing our traditional foods journey and weekly menu plans, showing how we rotated through 13 weeks of beans. Okay, there were a few other things in our diet, but it really was a lot of beans. You can still read those articles on my current blog, Homespun Oasis.

Amazingly, even with eating lots of beans, we all stopped having tummy troubles. There were many nourishing and nutrient-dense foods that were now a regular part of our diet. Bone broth was a staple in our kitchen. Fermented fruits and vegetables. Sourdough and soaked baked goods. So many wonderful and tasty dishes that were healing to our bodies.

The next summer, we raised meat birds for ourselves and others in the community. Homegrown chicken is amazing! And after watching the movie *Food, Inc.*, it's difficult for me to eat commercially raised chickens.

Even though we were dedicated to eating traditional foods, we weren't legalistic about it. Most of the food we brought into the home was real or whole, and most of the preparations were traditional. Grains were soaked, soured, or sprouted. We read labels and chose the best options our budget would allow.

For the most part, we rarely bought organics. I remember a blog post I wrote about a shopping trip—with plenty of pictures of my purchases—that someone shared to her Facebook page. My post was shredded in the comments because I'd shopped at a chain store and there were zero organics photographed. It didn't matter that the entire shopping trip was focused on purchasing food on a food-stamp budget and making the dollar stretch.

Our goal was to eat real, whole, traditional foods, focusing on the Weston A. Price Foundation Dietary Guidelines 80 percent of the time. The other 20 percent we weren't terribly strict about.

Of course, we didn't have any real way of tracking our 80/20 plan, but my body knew! When I'd slide a little too much toward the junk and processed foods, the tummy troubles would start up. To this day, I'm fine if I go out for dinner and eat anything I want that one time. But if I'm poorly eating several meals in a row, I suffer with a gut ache and overall fatigue.

In this book, you'll find many suggestions for no-cook foods that align perfectly with the Weston A. Price Foundation (WAPF) Dietary Guidelines. But very much like in my everyday life, my food storage is not strictly WAPF. We make provisions and allow for items not only on the Dietary Guidelines list but that make the WAPF's Dietary Dangers list.

There will be several times throughout this book where I'll make a note about something not meeting WAPF guidelines. If you are a dietary purist, you'll want to do your own research on whether to include these items in your no-cook food storage.

Prepping and traditional foods naturally led us to homesteading. We started on our two acres in Central Wyoming with chickens for eggs and then moved on to meat birds. A few years later, we added Nigerian Dwarf goats for milk and meat. We never did butcher any, but the milk was amazing. I was soon making yogurt, kefir, and cheeses.

In 2016, we moved to twenty acres in Northern Wyoming, building up from bare land. The first three and a half years we lived off the grid, without running water but with a small solar system and internet so I could work from home.

I've been a telecommuter since 2008, before it was the "thing" to do, working several part-time jobs with flexible hours, along with running my Homespun Oasis blog and writing traditional foods books. This gave us a lot of freedom to pursue our homesteading desires.

In 2019, I published my Christian Cozy Apocalyptic Fiction series using our off-grid, homesteading, preparedness, traditional foods lifestyle as a guide to what the end of the world may look like. The 12-book *Havoc in Wyoming* series is complete with a six-book spin off series, *Montana Mayhem*. A new spin off series will be released in 2023.

Why No-Cook?

Most of us spend a good part of our day preparing and consuming food. And many of us spend a big portion of time *thinking* about food. Planning what to eat for three meals plus snacks, day in and day out, is part of our conditioning. We may try and make that easier on ourselves with a menu plan so the "heavy thinking" is cut down to once a week or even once a month, but food is still essential.

Sure, most of us could go without food for several days. In the generally accepted rules of three for survival, food falls lowest on the list.

- You can survive for three minutes without air (oxygen) or in icy water
- You can survive for three hours without shelter in a harsh environment (unless in icy water)
- You can survive for three days without water (if sheltered from a harsh environment)
- You can survive for three weeks without food (if you have water and shelter)

Three weeks without food may be a minimal amount for some. I know people who've done prolonged liquid fasts for religious or weight loss reasons, well beyond the three weeks. But in those cases, often they are under a doctor's care or adding special electrolytes to their tea or water. Possibly, their liquid diet is even smoothies, shakes, or other calorie-laden beverages.

While it may be possible to survive for three weeks without food, it may not be comfortable. Setting up a simple plan, and adding the basic kinds of foods you eat today, is an easy way to stay comfortable in a short- or long-term situation.

During our eye-opening gale storm event, we did fine by eating from the fridge and low-stocked freezer, then moving on to simple canned goods. Our all-electric house didn't have a cooking (or heating) option, but we did have a couple of camp stoves and fuel. That said, had the power outage continued for any real length of time, we would've been in trouble.

That experience, which led my family to the world of preparedness, also led us to create what I affectionately dubbed "The Heat and Eat Bin." This was simply a lidded tote filled with easy-to-cook and no-cook foods to last us at least a week. Since the contents of the bin were shelf-stable cans and some dried goods, they weren't necessarily Weston A. Price style foods, but I did scour the ingredient lists to choose the most nutritious items possible.

The thought behind this bin was a week of food would be more than enough for a power outage, especially since we would do our best to empty the fridge first. We'd keep the freezer closed and cover it with quilts, then run the generator a few times a day to keep everything frozen. This bin could also do double duty as a quick meal option for times I was sick or hadn't planned a meal.

During that time, we were a family of five living at home. One bin held more than a week's worth of food for all of us. Also, during that time, our two oldest college-aged daughters were drifting in and out or living nearby, so we kept a second stocked bin with more food and cooking necessities, such as manual can openers, a single-burner camp stove, a one-pound propane bottle, a cooking pot, and a teakettle. Adding these items made the bins portable in case we needed to leave home in a hurry. The need for evacuation did *nearly* happen two times in those years, both because of wildfires.

Now there's just three of us at home; my husband, young teenage son, and me. We've swapped out the large bins for reusable grocery bags kept packed and ready to go, but with slightly different options from those early days.

Now our "to go" food focuses on no-cook items with a few quick-cooking or low-cook things added in. We've also swapped our large, one-burner, propane camp stove for a small backpacking stove that uses isobutane (a combination of butane and propane that comes in small containers) to cut down on weight and space needs.

These evacuation food bags were put to use several months back when a massive windstorm swept through our area, resulting in a fast-moving wildfire in the middle of the night. With our go-bags at the ready, we spent only mere minutes loading the cars with our supplies and pets.

After reaching a friend's home that was safely outside of the evacuation zone, along with several other families, we started comparing the items we grabbed on our way out the door. We were the only ones who thought of things like food and a change of clothes. On that windy night, I think many people realized the need for an emergency evacuation bag.

While this isn't a book about 72-hour bags (also called FEMA bags or bug-out bags), many of the food ideas will lend themselves to these types of needs. They're also ideas we use for our get-home bags. You can find links to more information on bug-out bags (BOBs) and get-home bags (GHBs) in the Resources section.

The Heat and Eat Bin, BOBs, and GHBs are all good reasons to turn to no-cook foods. Not only are they convenient but they also save on fuel costs. Hunkering down at home offers its own need for the same foods.

Like in my case during the gale, if you live in an all-electric home when the power goes out, you need alternative ways to cook. Most of those ways will use some form of fuel. If the power is out due to downed trees or a major snowstorm, you won't want to run to the sporting goods store to buy another bottle of propane just so you can heat up your soup up on the grill.

And if stores are also without power, will they even be open? Plan ahead now for alternative cooking methods during a power outage, and keep a reasonable amount of your needed fuel safely stored.

While I have mainly discussed storms and other reasons you may experience a short-term power outage, there's always the possibility of long-term issues. A week without power felt like a long time, but other events have resulted in much longer outages. Devastation from a hurricane may mean weeks or even months before power is restored to everyone.

For years, people living in South Africa have experienced times of rolling blackouts. As I'm writing this, in the summer of 2022 (summer in the United States, winter in South Africa), they're on stage six of their rolling blackout schedule. This puts them at scheduled times without electricity for six to eight hours per day.

In the United States, power outages from severe storms have doubled over the past two decades thanks to our aging power grid. Essential power grid maintenance is skyrocketing in cost as utilities attempt to upgrade transmission lines and equipment. While there is some disagreement on why we're seeing severe weather changes, the power grid issues are here. We may not be to the rolling blackout stage of South Africa, but it's still something to keep an eye on.

Preparing for regional, statewide, or countrywide events is something to consider. Preparing for larger, worldwide events is also important. The war between Russia and Ukraine is one such matter. While we may not have fighting here, we're seeing the effects of it in the cost of fuel and groceries, plus threats of shortages.

In my opinion, there's more to it than the war between Russia and Ukraine, but this is widely pointed to as one reason for the predicted recession of 2022. During the Great Recession of 2008, unemployment peaked in October of 2009, reaching 11.1 percent for males, with women slightly lower (source 3).

Remember my friend I mentioned earlier? The one who lived on their food storage while her husband was out of work? This was during that time. Having food on hand took a great amount of stress off them. What if their food storage also contained a large amount of no-cook or low-cook items so they could not only keep their bellies full, but also cut their costs of electricity (or gas or propane/LPG) at the same time? The less money going out, the better, especially during a time when every penny may count.

With inflation increasing, many suggest we're entering another recession, and some say we're already there. Will we see high unemployment again? Since the Great Resignation began, where a record number of people have left their jobs since the beginning of the pandemic, it's hard to envision what the unemployment numbers may look like. With many people starting their own business or doing contract work, those numbers may not even be accurately counted.

But if it's you out of work—counted as unemployed or not—it may be an emergency situation. What can you do today to help with that possibility?

We've discussed a few common, and likely, reasons to add no-cook foods and recipes to your food storage. Other life-altering, wide-spread reasons exist and should be considered, such as the New Madrid Fault Earthquake, peak oil, financial collapse, World War III, electromagnetic pulse, and a whole host of other possibilities of varying likelihood. If you've ever caught an episode of *Doomsday Preppers*, you know the reasons people prep are endless.

Early in my days of preparedness, I had a good friend who was a longtime prepper and willing to show me the ropes. She taught me many necessary skills, including canning and caring for meat rabbits, plus provided hours of great conversation as we bounced around ideas. She was the person who sparked my interest in no-cook foods for my food storage.

Her reason for stocking no-cook foods was simple: food odors.

She lived in a populated area and was fully aware of how food odors travel. She also knew hungry people have extremely sensitive noses and are often willing to do whatever is necessary to relieve their hunger. While she did have regular, long-term, popular storage foods, she focused on what I've come to think of as guerrilla eating.

I suspect many of us have heard of guerrilla gardening, which is essentially planting hidden caches, and the idea of keeping rabbits for protein because they're quiet and don't require much space.

Guerrilla eating is the same concept: keeping no-cook or quick-cooking foods that have low odor. This is an idea you should consider if you live in a heavily populated area.

As you read through this book, use it as a starting point. You may think of many more ideas that would work well in your area for no-cook food storage options. You may think of other fuel-saving and low-odor cooking methods. Things that work well for me, in my rural Wyoming area, may not work well for you, but you may come up with the perfect solution with a little thought.

Be sure to check the Resources section at the end of this book. Many of the ideas I present will go into greater detail in other articles. There are plenty of links, book suggestions, and general information to further your knowledge.

Short-Term or Long-Term Storage?

We follow the motto of "store what you eat, eat what you store." While we do have some items that are packaged for long-term storage, sealed up and stowed on an out-of-the-way shelf, those are the exception and not the rule. And truthfully, those items are purchased with a plan in mind and are saved to use at "the end of the world as we know it."

We store what we eat by focusing on foods we know we enjoy. During a time when we were particularly strapped for cash, early in our preparedness journey, my husband and I set out on a quest to cut our grocery bill to the bare minimum while also focusing on nourishing foods that could fill our pantry.

Beans became the focus for most of our meals for over a year. When we started our "bean adventure," I was only familiar with pinto beans. As a child, my mom would make a big batch of pinto beans on Friday night along with a pan of cornbread. That became the basis of all our meals over the weekend.

I used that concept, combined with an idea from a blog I read (it no longer exists but was appropriately called Lentils and Rice), to learn all I could about cooking with beans. We would buy small quantities of different varieties, and I'd experiment with them. I'd make a big pot of beans and turn it into three or four meals. The bean varieties we enjoyed we'd buy in bulk (at a lower price per pound), not only for our food storage but to eat regularly.

By storing what we eat, we can follow our second motto of first in, first out (FIFO). Using FIFO, we regularly rotate our food storage to ensure we have the freshest items available and we're using certain goods by their best-by date.

While the best-by date is a recommendation of when foods should be consumed, most items don't spoil on the next day. Most shelf-stable items are fine to eat well past the date stamped on the can or package.

For canned goods, you should inspect the can thoroughly to make sure it's not bulging or damaged. Things like crackers or cereal may go stale after a time, but they are still safe. Foods in your freezer won't grow bacteria, so food poisoning isn't possible, though they could become freezer burned or have less flavor.

Beans and grains that have been properly packaged will keep indefinitely. Other foods suitable for indefinite storage include honey, salt, sugar, and instant coffee. These are the items we use as the foundation of our food storage—the long-term storage foods.

Keeping a variety of beans and grains on hand gives us many different tastes and flavors. Adding in herbs and spices as a layer of our food storage increases those tastes and flavors. While dried herbs don't have the "forever" shelf life of beans, they can keep for years when properly packaged and stored. Plus, herbs are easy to grow in the backyard, on a balcony, or even in a sunny window.

Canned foods, pasta, flour (as opposed to whole grains) and flour mixes (for cakes or biscuits), soup mixes, and other shelf-stable foods fall under the short-term storage list. Even though beans and grains are my foundation, these easy-to-acquire foods make up the majority of our food storage.

A can of tomatoes may not have the 20-year shelf life that a bucket of mylar-packaged beans has, but they're still good for several years (as long as the can isn't damaged) and, though low in calories, it will provide many nutrients and flavor. Adding a can of tomatoes and some chili powder to those humble beans gives a whole new flavor experience.

The nutrition in canned tomatoes is almost identical to fresh tomatoes, with the canned being higher in the antioxidant lycopene. Canned tomatoes can also be eaten without cooking, perfect for our no-cook needs.

I remember reading a story several years ago, early in my preparedness journey and most likely in some kind of forum or article, about a woman who was a child during the Great Depression. She and her family were displaced and traveling, living on nothing while barely surviving. I don't remember the details, but they were given a jar of canned tomatoes. The story went on to describe the pure glee they experienced while sharing those tomatoes and how it was the best food ever. That story convinced me to store a respectable number of canned tomatoes.

How much of these short-term storage items should you store? There're several detailed food storage calculators you can use to get an idea. While I like the basic food storage calculators for my long-term, bulk-purchased items, I don't use it for canned goods.

Sure, I can do the math to figure out how many cans of tomatoes I need to buy to equal ten pounds (the recommendation for one person for 52 weeks), but I've found it works better to decide how many times per week I use a can of tomatoes. In my house, on average, I use two cans of tomatoes each week. This is mainly during the winter when we're eating more soups and stews and don't have anything from the garden. Two cans per week translates to 104 cans for a one-year supply.

Side Note: Canned tomatoes are very low in calories. A half cup of canned tomatoes has only 39 calories, which won't go very far in giving your body the energy it needs to get through the day. Same with canned green beans, which is approximately 30 calories per half cup. Canned corn comes in much higher at 83 calories per half cup.

While keeping these vegetables (okay, yes, tomatoes are really a fruit, but we treat them as a vegetable) is smart for their use, taste, and nourishment, calories provide energy. Canned vegetables are low on the calorie scale. Something to think about is the calories your body needs to get through your day. We'll discuss this often as we move through our no-cook concepts.

I use a similar method for other canned goods like green beans, corn, salmon, tuna, peanut butter, and so on. Knowing the amount of these items we use during our regular life, and keeping the goods organized, helps with FIFO.

Another method I use for FIFO is marking on cans and boxes as they are brought in. When we come home from a shopping excursion, I empty all the grocery bags onto the table.

Once the refrigerator items are put away, I get out a Sharpie and mark the purchase month and year on all the frozen food before putting it away. Then I mark the month and year on all the cans. While some of the boxes or packages are marked and put in the pantry, others may need to be vacuum sealed before being labeled and put away. When putting away the shelf-stable and frozen foods, I try to move the new items to the back and pull the older items forward, just like a grocery store does.

Even though I'm pretty diligent with my Sharpie and my FIFO, things still slip by. To help combat this, once a year—usually the end of June or early July—we spend a weekend going through the pantry and cabinets. We set up folding tables in the living room and empty everything out. Invariably, we'll find things put in the wrong places, without Sharpie dates, or other issues.

Once the shelves are emptied, everything gets wiped down. We keep cotton balls with tea tree oil or eucalyptus in the pantry to help combat pests. These get replaced after the cleaning and are saturated with new oil. I refresh the cotton balls every month or so as needed. It's easy to tell when it's time because the scent begins to fade.

Once everything is cleaned, we check all of the cans and packages for damage and dates, then put everything back in place. If there are items with older Sharpie dates, I'll check the best-by date and pull them out to use sooner as needed. If Sharpie dates are missing on items, I'll estimate what the date should be based on similar best-by stamps of the same product.

After cleaning and organizing the pantry and cabinets, which house the majority of our short-term food storage (those shelf-stable items in cans and packages), we also check the long-term buckets and pails. We open the lids and check the mylar bag inside, ensuring it's still sealed and everything looks as it should.

Some of our buckets have multiple packs of smaller, one-gallon mylar bags or packages of vacuum-sealed goods. Each individual package is inspected. Although these items are packaged for long-term storage, they are not just packaged and forgotten. When we need beans in the kitchen, we shop our buckets first. If we need coconut shreds, we grab a vacuum-sealed package from a pail.

We tackle the freezers a few weeks later, emptying, defrosting, checking for dates, and making sure the packages look good. A good portion of our freezer food is home-raised and harvested chicken or wild game. Some years we'll have a surplus that we need to use up before the upcoming hunting season to make room. The surplus may be pressure canned or dehydrated (we still store dehydrated meat in the freezer, but it uses less space). Sometimes, I'll make freezer meals so we have ready-to-eat food for busy nights.

I'll admit, this yearly cleaning and inspection is a big job and takes some time. But for the peace of mind it gives, we'll keep doing it.

As you build your food storage, no matter if it's no-cook or for regular ol' cooking, you should also develop a way to ensure you are storing what you eat and eating what you store, plus using the oldest items first. Use this concept for both your short-term and long-term storage, replacing and repurchasing as needed, and you'll not only have the freshest food possible, but you'll also save money in the long run.

Herbs, Spices, Sweeteners, and Sauces

I absolutely love having a large selection of seasonings and spices on hand. While none of these items are likely to provide enough calories to sustain you, keeping herbs, spices, and sauces as part of your food storage will be a huge benefit for all your meals, whether using a specific cooking method or not.

By keeping a variety of different spices, I can easily change the flavors of our meals and create new dishes. When planning no-cook or minimal-cook meals, the change in flavors can really make a difference in your enjoyment.

A word of caution, while I love pungent spices like curry, if low odor is your goal, curry may not be the best choice. Even a low simmer releases all the curry goodness in taste and aroma. Save the curry for adding to sauces and dips that don't need to be cooked, or sprinkle it on items after cooking.

We don't buy those little jars of spices in the grocery store. Not only are they overpriced, but they're also almost always irradiated. The process of irradiation uses ionized radiation to increase shelf life and kill bacteria. This leaves a "dead" product with zero medicinal qualities.

Many herbs and spices have historically doubled as medicine. Ginger can help with nausea and reduce pain. Turmeric and black pepper are anti-inflammatories, fresh garlic has antibiotic properties, and the list goes on. Having the freshest, highest-quality items may be helpful overall.

We buy most of our spices through Azure Standard because they are not irradiated, and also because their bulk pricing is quite good. We've also found some great spices in our local health food store and online from Frontier Co-op.

If you're unsure of the flavor of a certain spice or seasoning, I recommend that you try a small quantity first before buying it by the pound. Purchasing a pound of a spice you like only so-so is not cost effective.

Keeping herbs, spices, sweeteners, and sauces as part of your food storage will be a huge benefit for all your meals for any style of cooking or no-cook methods.

The Basics

Start your seasoning stock with the basics: sea salt and ground black pepper.

Storing sea salt is not only easy, it's smart. Have you read *Alas, Babylon* by Pat Frank? I have (many times), and the town running out of salt made a huge impression on me! So much so, we've chosen to go well above the popular food calculator guidelines of six pounds per person per year in our storeroom.

We prefer Redmond's Sea Salt and stock up when it goes on sale, plus we also buy 50-pound bags of Redmond's #4 animal salt. We use it for our livestock but know it'll be fine for human consumption if needed.

Keep your sea salt clean and dry. If your salt does get slightly wet, you can allow it to dry and it'll be good as new (you may lose some due to dissolving).

Non-iodized salt does not contain added iodine, a necessary mineral our body doesn't make. All salts do contain some naturally occurring iodine, but not enough to meet the Recommended Daily Allowance (RDA) of 150 micrograms per day (women who are pregnant or breastfeeding need more than the RDA). Canned and processed foods, though often high in salt, also use salts without iodine.

Iodine is essential for a healthy thyroid, metabolism, and more. Since it isn't artificially added to the sea salt we purchase and store, we look for iodine in other sources. Seafood, kelp (nori), plants grown near the sea, dairy products, and eggs are all natural sources. One easy option for adding iodine is seasoning dishes with ground kelp.

There are also supplements like Lugol's 2% solution, which is an easy option for meeting your iodine needs. For most people, a couple of drops on the skin daily will keep your thyroid functioning properly. Lugol's 2% solution is also an option to use for prevention of radiation poisoning (source 5) and is a fabulous item to consider for your medical supply cabinet.

Ground black pepper has a shelf life of about six months, officially. I'll admit, I keep mine much longer than this! I buy it in bulk packages and refill my container. The rest is vacuum sealed in small quantities and used as needed. Black peppercorns can also be used and ground fresh as needed. These do have a longer shelf life of one to three years, depending on who you ask.

Spices and Herbs

After you have your salt and pepper sorted out, add in other spices you use regularly. Here are a few ideas. Spices with an asterisk (*) next to them are included in at least one recipe in this book. Salt and pepper are listed in nearly all recipes. Also, even though I'm listing garlic in this section, botanically it's considered a vegetable. Onion, however, is classified as an herb.

- Cumin*
- Chili powder*
- Cayenne pepper*
- Garlic powder or granules*
- Onion powder

- Dehydrated minced onion
- Turmeric
- Ground coriander
- Ground ginger★
- Mustard powder
- Curry powder★
- Cinnamon
- Nutmeg
- Paprika
- Smoked paprika★
- Dried pepper flakes★
- Dried parsley★
- Dried basil
- Dried oregano★ (I keep both regular, sometimes called Italian or Mediterranean, and Mexican oregano because the flavors are different)
- Dried sage
- Dried dill★
- Dried cilantro flakes★ (sometimes called dried coriander flakes)

We built these up slowly, adding one or two per month as our budget allowed. To store these, we vacuum sealed them in two- to four-ounce packages. We use a lot of curry powder, so we do that in a four-ounce package. We use very little nutmeg, so it gets a smaller bag.

If you grow or wildcraft herbs, still consider adding a stash of dried ones. Anything could happen to your garden supply. About 10 years ago, we had a terrible grasshopper infestation. Within a matter of hours, everything green was whittled to the ground.

Plus, since the subject of this book is essentially guerrilla eating— preparing food without anyone knowing about it—it makes sense you may not be spending much time in the garden or walking around looking for wild edibles.

Sweeteners

Also helpful for flavoring are sweeteners. I wrestled with giving them their own category in this book, but in my life we do very little baked goods and use limited amounts of sweeteners.

While I do store pure cane sugar, Sucanat (natural cane sugar), honey, molasses, stevia, and a few other sweeteners, they are truly used more like a spice—added to liven things up. A few times a year, I bake a cake (preferably sourdough!) or will make a pie or other decadent item as a treat.

Since this book focuses on no-cook items, I've left out the sourdough cake and pumpkin pie. Instead, I've included a few nutrient-dense recipes that may have a splash of sweet in them.

If you follow a food calculator, the recommendation is 60 pounds per person, per year. Some calculators include jam and Jell-O in this amount.

Stevia is a sweetener I don't see listed on food calculators, but it's highly used in my kitchen. Made from the leaves of the stevia plant, it's over 100 times sweeter than sugar but has zero carbs. It also has a weird aftertaste! I don't find the taste to be unpleasant now, but I wasn't too sure when I first tried it. Remember, a little goes a long way with stevia.

Here are a few ideas on sweeteners for your food storage. Those with an asterisk (*) next to them are included in at least one recipe in this book.

- Pure cane sugar
- Sucanat or Rapadura (unrefined, natural cane sugar high in molasses)
- Honey* (it is sweeter than other natural sweeteners, so I use half as much honey as sugar or maple syrup)
- Blackstrap molasses (a good source of iron, calcium, magnesium, potassium, and phosphorus)

24

- Maple syrup★
- Coconut sugar
- Coconut syrup
- Stevia★ (I keep both pure liquid, to use by the drop, and a granulated blend that includes organic erythritol)
- Monk fruit (Lo Han/Luo Han, a low-carb sweetener that's gaining in popularity)
- Jams, jellies, and preserves
- Dried or freeze-dried fruits★
- Fruit powder(s)★

Sauces

Here's a big flavor opportunity! For our purposes, I'm going to be rather generous with what I consider a sauce. There are going to be things I mention where you'll screw up your face and think, "That's not a sauce." I know . . . but consider adding it to your food storage anyway, because if I'm listing it, there's a reason. It just might be the secret ingredient that makes your no-cook dish sing.

Sauces with an asterisk (★) next to them are included in at least one recipe in this book.

- Soy sauce
- Coconut aminos
- Fish sauce
- Worcestershire sauce
- Liquid smoke★
- A variety of hot and chili sauces (Sriracha★, Cholula, sweet chili sauce, tabasco, wing sauce, etc.)
- Lemon juice★
- Lime juice
- Apple cider vinegar
- Assorted flavored vinegars★ (balsamic, red wine, white wine, etc.)
- Mustard★ (regular, Dijon, grained, etc.)

- Ketchup
- Marinara sauce
- Tomato sauce
- Other commercially available sauces you enjoy, such as hoisin, pad Thai, vodka pasta sauce, etc.
- Tomato powder and tomato flakes (to make ketchup, tomato sauce, marinara, and a ton of other things)
- Sour cream powder
- Egg yolk powder

One sauce you might notice missing from my list is mayonnaise. I'll admit, I love mayo. You can certainly add mayo to your list, but be aware the best-by date is usually six months or less. I've opened a long-expired mayo before, and that's an experience I never want to repeat!

We do purchase mayo but prefer to make our own. Most commercial mayonnaise is made from soy oil, something we are trying to limit our consumption of. I've tried a few of the olive oil mayonnaises and am not a fan.

But I am a huge fan of homemade mayo! If you have access to farm-fresh eggs, store the ingredients to make your mayo. It's so good! Don't have farm-fresh eggs? Store egg yolk powder for a decent mayo replacement.

The key to a nice, thick mayonnaise is emulsification. Room temperature ingredients, plus not rushing, will give you the thickest mayo. Being able to control your mixture is also important. Here's my favorite recipe and method.

No Electricity Required Mayonnaise

- ⅓ cup olive oil
- ⅓ cup avocado oil
- ⅓ cup coconut oil (in its liquid state but not hot)
- 1 egg yolk (preferably free-range, room temperature)
- 1 teaspoon Dijon mustard★
- 1 tablespoon lemon juice (or apple cider vinegar)
- Sea salt, to taste
- Ground black pepper, to taste (optional)

Combine the oils in a glass measuring cup with a pour spout.

Place the egg yolk and mustard in a glass bowl. Choose a size larger than you think you need. You'll be adding the oil and whisking as you go. Whisk together the egg yolk and mustard until smooth.

Now here's the key to good emulsification. You're going to whisk with one hand while slowly (a few drops at a time) adding the oil with the other hand and blending well as you go.

27

Alternatively, you can add a few drops of oil, stop pouring, blend well, then add a few more drops. It's important to make sure the oil is completely mixed in before adding too much.

If you go too fast with your oil, your mayo will break. Not the end of the world, but it won't be the lovely, thick sauce you want.

Once all the oil is added, it should be thick like frosting. Add the lemon juice (or apple cider vinegar) and whisk to combine. Give it a taste, then season with salt and pepper. Voilà! Perfect mayo with minimal ingredients and no electricity needed.

Let's talk about olive oil for mayo. High-quality extra-virgin olive oil is often very robust. I love the flavor of it for many things but find it to be a little much in mayonnaise, which is one reason I cut the extra-virgin olive oil (EVOO) with avocado and coconut oil. I still save my best EVOO for other uses and reach for a milder version.

If you don't have avocado oil, feel free to use ⅔ cup olive oil and ⅓ cup coconut oil. If you only have olive oil, use 100 percent olive oil but know the flavor may be a little stronger than anything you purchase in the store. I love the addition of coconut oil in this because it firms up nicely when cooled.

On the flip side, coconut oil is liquid above 77°. Keeping your mayo in warm temperatures will cause it to liquify. Consider this if you find yourself without refrigeration.

What if the mayo broke? You can try and salvage a broken or split mayo with an additional room temperature egg yolk. Whisk the yolk in a bowl, and slowly (a tablespoon or so at a time) add the broken mayo to the fresh yolk, whisking between each addition. It should re-emulsify.

*The mustard also helps with the emulsifying process. You can use regular instead of Dijon if you prefer. Once you are comfortable with making mayo, you can omit the mustard. I rarely add it now. I like the mustard-free flavor better.

Powdered Egg Yolk Mayo

Powdered egg yolk is a useful food storage item. Powdered egg yolk is (most commonly) pasteurized yolks that have been spray dried. It has a long shelf life (years) and can be used in just about any recipe that calls for fresh yolks. It does emulsify well . . . until it doesn't.

I find this mayonnaise to work best using the three oils—olive, avocado, and coconut (in its liquid state). It whisks nicely until about ⅔ cup of oil and then starts to thin and break. I've tried it using less oil, but the eggy flavor was too strong for me. The ⅓ cup of coconut oil thickens just enough when chilled to make a nice mayo consistency.

I haven't tried it, but I think bacon grease would also be a great "oil" for this mayonnaise in place of the coconut oil. The bacon flavor would shine through while providing enough thickness when chilled. If using bacon grease, you want it liquid but not hot. Mix it well with the olive and avocado oils.

Reconstitute the egg yolk powder in a medium bowl. With all the whisking needed, this is most certainly a time you should use a larger bowl than you think you'll need. Otherwise, you may end up with egg everywhere.

- ⅓ cup olive oil
- ⅓ cup avocado oil
- ⅓ cup coconut oil, in its liquid state but not hot
- Egg yolk powder, reconstituted with water to equal one yolk★
- 1 teaspoon Dijon mustard
- 1 tablespoon lemon juice, plus additional★★
- Sea salt, to taste
- Ground black pepper, to taste

Combine the oils in a glass measuring cup with a pour spout.

To the reconstituted egg yolk, add the mustard and whisk until smooth. Add the lemon juice about ⅓ at a time, whisking between additions. I just drizzle a little in, whisk until smooth, then drizzle again until all the lemon juice is incorporated. The egg yolk powder tends to clump, so the slow additions help with this. Adding the lemon juice before the oil provides much better emulsification and a smoother mayo.

After everything is blended, I add a few pinches of sea salt and blend again. I think the egg yolk powder mayo needs more salt than fresh yolk mayo, and I like adding the salt in stages.

Now that you have a smooth, well-blended batter, it's time to add the oil. Whisk with one hand while slowly (a few drops at a time) adding the oil with the other hand and blending well as you go.

Alternatively, you can add a few drops of oil, stop pouring, blend well, then add a few more drops. It's important to make sure the oil is completely mixed in before adding too much.

With proper emulsification, the mayo will be nice and thick until you have only about ⅓ cup of oil left, then it tends to become thin. Keep slowly adding the oil and mixing.

When all the oil is in, move the mayo to the fridge or another cool place to allow the coconut oil to thicken, which will then thicken the mayonnaise. Once it's the consistency of a thick batter, remove it from the fridge and give it a gentle stir.

Taste and adjust salt and pepper as needed. You may also wish to add additional lemon juice. I don't think my fresh egg mayo needs more than a tablespoon, but the powdered egg has a better flavor with extra lemon juice, and the consistency is improved. I add it 1 teaspoon at a time, blending and sampling as I go.

Once the flavors are to your liking, transfer the mayo to a lidded jar and keep in a cold place until ready to use.

*Follow the instructions included with your powdered egg yolk product to reconstitute to equal one egg.

**You could use apple cider vinegar instead of lemon juice. I find the lemon juice flavor more pleasing with the powdered egg product, especially since it seems to need more than the fresh egg yolk mayo.

Mayonnaise Variations

Homemade mayonnaise makes a great vehicle for a variety of sauces, dips, and dressings. In minutes, I can whip up a ranch or coleslaw dressing, or any number of tasty condiments. Even just stirring in a little curry powder and lime juice gives a whole new flavor experience. Here are a few of my favorite mayo-based sauces.

Sriracha Mayo

This is one of my absolute favorites! It's spectacular on homemade sushi (check out my book *Sprouts for Your Food Storage* for my son's favorite sushi roll using canned tuna, and also see Tuna Rolls in the Seeds chapter of this book), sandwiches, burgers, or even as a sauce for rice noodles. For a different variation and flavor, use your favorite hot sauce, such as Cholula, wing sauce, or even tabasco.

- ½ cup mayonnaise (real yolk or powdered)
- 1 teaspoon to 1 tablespoon Sriracha sauce (maybe more if you like the spice)

- A few dashes of soy sauce or sea salt to taste

Combine, taste, adjust if needed, and enjoy!

Tartar Sauce

- ½ cup mayonnaise (real yolk or powdered)
- 1 small dill pickle, finely minced
- 1 tablespoon lemon juice
- 1 teaspoon dried dill
- 1 teaspoon dried minced onion
- 1 teaspoon Worcestershire sauce
- Sea salt, to taste
- Ground black pepper, to taste

Combine mayonnaise, minced pickle, lemon juice, dried dill, dried minced onion, and Worcestershire sauce. Stir until mixed thoroughly. Taste, then add sea salt and pepper as needed.

Set aside for at least 30 minutes, allowing the flavors to meld and the dill and onions to reconstitute.

Creamy Cocktail Sauce

- ½ cup mayonnaise (real yolk or powdered)
- 2 tablespoons ketchup (or tomato sauce)
- 1 tablespoon lemon juice
- 1 tablespoon Worcestershire sauce
- 1 to 2 tablespoons prepared horseradish (how hot do you like it?)
- ¼ teaspoon garlic powder
- 1 to 4 dashes hot sauce (optional)
- Sea salt, to taste
- Ground black pepper, to taste

Mix mayonnaise and ketchup until smooth. Stir in lemon juice, Worcestershire sauce, horseradish, and garlic powder and then taste for seasonings. Does it need hot sauce? Salt? Pepper? Add if desired.

Aioli

This is dreamy goodness! To make aioli even better, use lemon juice instead of apple cider vinegar when making the mayo. The addition of a little more lemon juice and garlic changes the mayo into this amazing sauce. It's perfect for dipping, drizzling, spooning over meats, fish, vegetables . . . just about anything! It's even fabulous as a pasta sauce—add extra oil to make it creamier if needed.

- 1 cup homemade mayo (real yolk or powdered)
- 2 cloves garlic, minced, or ½ teaspoon garlic powder
- 1 teaspoon olive oil
- 1 tablespoon lemon juice
- Sea salt, to taste
- Ground black pepper, to taste

In a medium bowl, combine mayo, garlic, olive oil, and lemon juice. Mix until creamy. Give it a taste, then sprinkle in a little salt and pepper.

Bang Bang Sauce

This sweet and spicy sauce is great for drizzling over fish, meat, or vegetables. It's also great as a dip for a variety of appetizers. It mixes up in minutes, with only a whisk or fork.

- 1 cup homemade mayo (real yolk or powdered)
- 3 tablespoons Sriracha
- ¼ cup sweet chili sauce
- 1 tablespoon maple syrup, ½ tablespoon honey, or a drop or two of liquid stevia
- 2 teaspoons garlic powder
- 1 teaspoon smoked paprika
- Sea salt, to taste
- Ground black pepper, to taste

Combine mayonnaise, Sriracha, sweet chili sauce, and sweetener in a bowl. Taste for sweetness and add additional if needed. Stir in garlic powder and smoked paprika. Taste again. Add salt and pepper as desired.

Traditional Fats

In my opinion, traditional fats are the most important item in my pantry. Fats are essential for your health. They help with brain function, enhance the immune system, help with leaky gut, and help you feel full longer, along with a whole other host of benefits. You need fats in your diet.

The type of fat you store is also important. You want to avoid rancid, fake fats. Grocery store shortening, canola, vegetable oil and the like are <u>fake fats</u> that will harm you instead of helping you. Pay particular attention if it says "heart healthy" on the package, because if it says that, it's probably not.

I suggest reading up on fats and what we have been led to believe about them. "The Oiling of America" from the Weston A. Price Foundation is a great article that details the trouble with fake fats. You'll find a link to this in the Resources section.

Good-quality fats are more expensive than their lesser-quality counterparts. Doing your best to concentrate your food storage dollars on fats will go a long way toward health and nutrition. I'd also highly suggest using these traditional, high-quality fats in your everyday life. Weed out the fake fats and replace them with healthy ones.

A few years ago, my family started multiday backpacking trips. During my research phase for these trips, I was surprised to learn that many hikers, especially those hiking long trails like the Appalachian Trail or Pacific Crest, make olive oil a regular part of their meals. Thinking about it, it makes total sense!

I recommend you make olive oil and other fats a regular ingredient in your no-cook food storage, and also know you can eat EVOO by the spoonful. A tablespoon of olive oil will provide 120 calories and 14 grams of fat. No carbs, fiber, or protein, but that fat will go a long way toward filling you up and giving you energy.

EVOO isn't the only fat you can consume straight. Avocado oil, coconut oil, MCT, and even animal fats like tallow can be eaten alone. Of course, looking for ways to add these fats into food is often more pleasing.

Just about any dish will benefit from a drizzle on top. I love combining hot water and coconut oil to make something that replicates cream for my hot cereal. The popular bulletproof coffee, which combines coffee, grass-fed butter, and MCT oil, is another way to add fat to your diet. If you don't have butter, substitute with coconut oil. Coconut oil is also a good substitute for the MCT oil.

If you're a coffee drinker, you probably have alternative ways of making coffee (French press, pour over, camp stove percolator) but keep in mind coffee smells amazing. The percolator is going to release the most aroma of the three, with the pour over releasing the least.

An option of even less wonderful coffee aroma is instant coffee. A bonus to instant coffee is the shelf life. You can vacuum seal it and it will keep just about forever, much longer than regular ground coffee or even whole beans.

Here's a list of fats I recommend for your no-cook food storage. Fats with an asterisk (★) next to them are included in at least one recipe in this book.

- Extra-virgin olive oil★
- Virgin olive oil★ (these are usually milder in flavor than EVOO; search out a high-quality brand)
- Expeller-pressed sesame oil
- Expeller-pressed flaxseed oil
- Coconut oil★ (I buy refined, which is unflavored, in bulk for daily use and unrefined, which retains the coconut flavor, in

smaller jars for occasional use; coconut oil is solid below 77° and begins to liquefy above that)

- Avocado oil*
- Palm oil
- Ghee and (maybe) butter
- Animal fats (we store these on the hoof)
- Cod liver oil
- Butter oil
- Peanut butter (a good source of fat)

Where to Purchase?

Fats are my most expensive pantry item. I've found that ordering in bulk (one- to five-gallon pails) is the cheapest way to purchase coconut oil. But it's still a chunk of change to put out at one time.

Sales or free shipping really helps with the cost. For years I purchased from a seller that had regular sales on their five-gallon pails. Then their prices went up and their sales stopped. Now I purchase by the gallon.

I order olive oil and avocado oil by the gallon. Again, I use sales or free shipping. I've also started storing ghee. I love cooking with it, and it has an excellent shelf life. When I find a great deal on butter, I stash a few extra pounds in the freezer. We'll talk more later about freezer storage specifically.

For other animal fats, you could contact local farmers/ranchers to see about getting fat to render yourself into tallow/lard. Making friends with farmers/ranchers can be very beneficial in helping you stock your pantry for less!

Peanut Butter Fat Cups

While a spoonful of EVOO will provide needed fat to help you feel full, you can also get the fat in a highly flavored treat. Fat bombs are popular in the keto world as a between-meal snack to help you feel full, keep you in ketosis, and provide a dessert-like treat.

For a true keto version, use natural unsweetened peanut butter and use monk fruit, erythritol, or stevia as your sweetener. Each cup is approximately 200 calories, 20 grams of fat, just under 6 grams of protein, and about 7 carbohydrates when using 1 tablespoon of honey as the sweetener. Carbs drop to 5 grams when using ½ teaspoon of monk fruit (this is my preferred sweetener and amount for this recipe).

- 1 cup peanut butter
- ½ cup coconut oil (preferably soft but not in its liquid state)
- ¼ cup unsweetened cocoa powder
- ¼ teaspoon sea salt
- Sweetener, to taste

In a muffin tin, add liners or coat with coconut oil, butter, or other traditional fat. Set aside.

In a medium bowl, combine peanut butter, coconut oil, cocoa powder, and sea salt until well blended.

Add your sweetener of choice. If using a granulated sweetener, like cane sugar or Sucanat, use a blender or coffee mill to make it into a fine powder. Start with less sweetener than you think you need and adjust up. You can combine different sweeteners if you prefer, using half powdered sugar and a few drops of stevia, for example. Make it work for you!

Once the flavors are how you wish and the batter is smooth, drop about two tablespoons into each muffin tin, being sure to use all the batter and fill all tins. Put in a cool place until set and solid (fridge or freezer work best, but anywhere cool is helpful).

Lemon Fat Bomb Bars

Looking for something fresh and wonderful? Try these Lemon Fat Bomb Bars. These use dried lemon peel powder for their amazing flavor. Be sure to check the Resources section on how to make your own lemon peel powder. It's super easy and makes a fabulous addition to your food storage.

This recipe makes 20 bite-sized servings, with each bar having approximately 170 calories and 13 grams of fat. When using just under ½ cup of honey, they have about 11 grams of carbs and 1 gram of protein.

My son says these remind him of rice crispy treats. He loves the amount of sweetener as written; I prefer less sweet and, if making them for myself only, use about half as much. This recipe works best using a sticky sweetener like honey or maple syrup. Keep in mind, honey is the sweeter of the two, so you can use less.

- 3 cups unsweetened shredded coconut

- 1 tablespoon lemon peel powder or 1 to 2 tablespoons lemon zest
- ½ teaspoon lemon extract
- ⅔ cup coconut oil (preferably soft but not in its liquid state)
- ¼ teaspoon sea salt
- Scant ½ cup honey or ¾ cup maple syrup

Line an 8 x 8 square pan with parchment paper or coat with coconut oil, butter, or other traditional fat.

In a large bowl, combine all ingredients and mix well. Transfer the batter to the prepared pan and press firmly into place.

Put in a cool place until set and solid (fridge or freezer work best).

When firm, cut bars into 20 small pieces. If your temps are over 77°, the coconut oil will be very soft to runny. Feel free to scoop out servings with a spoon and enjoy.

Dairy and Dairy Alternatives

Milk has been described as a nearly perfect food. With protein, calcium, and vitamins, along with essential amino acids, it's possible to survive on milk alone. Not only survive, but thrive.

The popular Raw Milk Diet, or Milk Cure, has people consuming quarts of raw milk each day and healing allergies, malnutrition, digestion issues, and even diseases. Some may add in a little raw cheese, but most "eat" only their milk for the duration of the healing time.

As the name implies, milk in the Raw Milk Diet is raw and preferably high quality from cows raised on pasture and fed what cows are meant to eat—grass. Ideally, our no-cook food storage will include a cow, goat, sheep, or even water buffalo for providing milk in times of an emergency. Realistically, that's not feasible for most.

I had a small herd of Nigerian Dwarf goats for many years. Last fall, the loss of our young buck, combined with drought and the loss of our hay source, brought my husband and I to the hard decision of rehoming our herd.

Nigerian Dwarfs are a dairy breed yet much smaller than other goats. Their smaller size makes them easy keepers and eliminates some of the popular goat concerns. Goats are notorious for escaping their fencing, but our goats rarely got out, and when they did, it was because a gate hadn't been properly secured or a fence panel had come loose.

Because of their small size, Nigerian Dwarfs don't give as much milk as a larger more popular dairy breed. Saanens, a full-size dairy goat, may give up to 2½ gallons of milk per day, whereas a Nigerian Dwarf gives only ½ gallon.

The butterfat in goats' milk can range from 1 to 10 percent, with Nigerian Dwarfs having the highest content. Butterfat is important for making cheese, and also results in a creamier milk flavor. Unlike cow milk, goat milk is naturally homogenized. As the milk sits, if there's a layer of cream that rises to the top, it's minimal.

Keeping and milking our own goats did give us an added measure of security. Without the goats, we've been reworking our food storage plans as far as dairy is concerned.

While raw unprocessed milk may be the perfect food, the milk sold in grocery stores (pasteurized and homogenized), along with shelf-stable ultra-high temperature pasteurized boxed milk and powdered milks, are not the same . . . not even close.

We've been taught pasteurization is essential for preventing infectious disease and illness. Unfortunately, it's not a guarantee. The 1985 Salmonella Outbreak, which sickened thousands and resulted in at least one death, was traced back to pasteurized 2 percent milk.

Raw milk from healthy dairy animals that eat a traditional diet of green grasses (either on pasture or baled for winter use), plus proper cleanliness and sanitation measures, has a low likelihood of disease.

Raw milk contains lactic-acid-producing bacteria that protects against pathogens. Pasteurization destroys these helpful organisms. The heat of pasteurization also alters amino acids, making the proteins less available. It also promotes rancidity of unsaturated fatty acids and the destruction of vitamins and enzymes.

After pasteurization, chemicals may be added to suppress odor and restore taste. Synthetic vitamins are added. And the milk is homogenized—the fat droplets are emulsified so the cream does not separate. After all that, powdered milk is added back to skim, 1 percent, and 2 percent varieties.

Commercial dehydration methods oxidize the cholesterol in powdered milk and create large quantities of cross-linked proteins, nitrate compounds, and free glutamic acid. All of these have the potential to cause harmful effects to the body, from toxicity to artery issues to carcinogenic concerns (source 2).

With the troubles of pasteurization, homogenization, and commercial dehydration, where does that leave those of us without our own raw milk source when choosing the healthiest dairy possible? Especially if we are looking for dairy options for our food storage?

Looking back in history, the process of fermentation or souring milk was found in almost all cultures that kept dairy herds. Products such as cultured butter and buttermilk, yogurt, kefir, clabber milk, and cheese—both hard and soft—have been used for centuries as not only nourishing foods but ways to extend the shelf life of fresh dairy.

Using this concept of traditional fermented and cultured dairy, we're cobbling together a no-cook food storage plan.

Part of our plan includes waxed cheese. Hard cheeses, such as high-quality cheddar, Swiss, and Parmesan, can be cut into small blocks and waxed to create a shelf-stable product.

Please do your own research on which hard cheeses to use and use the proper cheese wax, not paraffin or other types of wax. (I wouldn't wax mass-produced cheddar or Swiss; it isn't dry enough.) I have several links in the Resources section, including a caution on not waxing cheese.

In addition to waxing cheese, we dehydrate dairy products. While cheese is too high in fat to safely dehydrate at home (see note at end of chapter), I'm comfortable with dehydrating yogurt.

I've dehydrated full-fat yogurt but choose to use nonfat for longer-term storage. Unfortunately, the issues with skim and low-fat milks mentioned above are also prevalent in their yogurt counterparts. Even so, this is a choice we've made to include dehydrated yogurt—sometimes called yogurt drops or yogurt bark—in our food storage.

I use a popular brand made with only skim milk and culture. I do take some solace in the company pledging to use milk made from non-GMO-fed cows. *Some solace.* Not a lot. Check the Resources for a link on how to make yogurt bark.

Another non-traditional food compromise we make is to store a small amount of full-fat commercially dried milk. According to the USDA's Food Saver App, powdered milk has a shelf life of three to five years if unopened, and it should be used within three months after opening. There is a caveat: the three- to five-year timetable is based on cool temperatures and dark storage. It may spoil as quickly as three months in hot temperatures. But this guide doesn't specify nonfat or full-fat. Since nonfat is the most popular powdered milk, I suspect the guideline reflects this.

Because fat can cause rancidity, I choose to err on the side of caution and keep only a limited supply of our full-fat dried milk. And we wouldn't store any if we didn't use it in our daily life.

Nonfat powdered milk is very popular in food storage. My favorite food storage calculator recommends 30 pounds of dairy (powdered milk, cheese powder, canned cheese, etc.) per person, per year. Because we don't use that much dried milk in a year, we don't store anywhere near that amount.

If you choose to store nonfat powdered milk, you can easily store those amounts due to the extended shelf life. For us, we use one 3.52-pound container of full-fat powdered milk about every four months. I've found, in my location and with my storage system, unopened jars are fresh well past their best-by date. Based on experience and our usage, we keep four containers on hand, which is only 14 pounds. We make up the rest of our dairy via other sources.

While I'm not a fan of powdered milk, it does come in handy on hiking, backpacking, and camping trips when regular milk would be an issue. I make shake 'em up smoothies in advance for a quick breakfast or snack on the trail. These are tasty no-cook protein-style drinks that will never meet the Weston A. Price Foundation standards, but they fall within our personal 80/20 rules of a traditional real food diet. I also use powdered milk for the occasional baking or cooking project when it's already going to be exposed to high temps and raw milk would be ruined.

Yogurt and kefir can be made from powdered milk. I'd like to think that by introducing the healthy live cultures and bacteria that are abundant in both yogurt and kefir starters, I'm undoing some of the damage of the commercial drying process. I could simply be fooling myself, but I'm leaning on this line from the book *Nourishing Traditions*: "If you cannot find good-quality raw milk, you should limit your consumption of milk products to cultured milk, cultured buttermilk, whole milk yoghurt, butter, cream and raw cheeses . . ." (source 2).

Making my own yogurt at home, using a live culture and dry milk, has worked out well. While everyone has heard of yogurt, kefir is still unfamiliar to some; although, it's gained in popularity in recent years.

Milk kefir is a little like yogurt, but it's usually drinkable and often tart. It can be slightly fizzy, but not always. Milk kefir is made with kefir grains, sometimes called a mother culture. The grains are symbiotic colonies of healthy bacteria and yeast that increase gut health, much like yogurt.

I love kefir for many reasons. Not only does it taste great and have wonderful healing properties, but it's sustainable. The kefir grains are not only reusable, but they grow during use. I once started with a tablespoon of grains added to my goat milk and then, over the course of several months, I soon had half a cup! In a long-term emergency situation, these growing grains could benefit many families.

I purchase kefir grains (not the kefir powder, which isn't sustainable) from Cultures for Health. Their grains are grown in pasteurized whole milk so whole milk is needed to rehydrate them. Once rehydrated, it's easy to convert the grains to use in rehydrated powdered milk. I haven't attempted rehydrating the grains in dry powdered milk, but that may work.

Do you know what else can be made from yogurt and kefir? Yogurt or kefir cheese! The wonderful soft cheese can be left plain with only salt or can have fresh or dried herbs added. The cheese can even be made extra dry and turned into cheese balls, which can be stored in olive oil for longer-term storage of several weeks.

This wonderful recipe is something I learned from Wardee at Traditional Cooking School in her Cultured Dairy & Basic Cheese eCourse. While Wardee uses raw milk from cows or goats in her recipes, the class is excellent for learning the procedures. I've also seen articles on making butter, ricotta, and a queso blanco style cheese. I've added links in the Resources section.

I also compromise by keeping powdered sour cream on hand. Like powdered milk, I keep only as much as we can use in a reasonable amount of time. It's another great hiking and camping item. I also reach for it when we're out of my favorite Daisy Sour Cream. Even though the powdered brand I choose suffers from the same processing issues as dried milk, the ingredient list is short and not terrible.

Because we keep a limited supply of shelf-stable dairy on hand, we also store dairy alternatives. Canned coconut milk is our main choice for cooking and baking. Coconut milk powder also works well for these and can be blended into a smoothie with a blender bottle, a battery-operated frother, or a whisk and strong arm. Because of the fat content in coconut milk powder, this is another item you should use for food storage.

You may also want to look into storing shelf-stable nut, oat, or rice milks. Because of the processing and additives, we prefer to limit our consumption of these items and rarely use them in our daily life, so we don't store them. We had to draw a line somewhere in our food rules!

I've also found that water combined with MCT oil, collagen, and a dash of sea salt is a good substitute for milks in beverages. This is a variation on Foundation Milk from the *Trim Healthy Mama Cookbook*. When we have smoothies, this is my favorite "milk" to use.

In addition for use in cooking and as a beverage, a big reason for dairy is the calcium. Our bones, teeth, and soft tissues need calcium. Our bodies can't produce calcium; we need to get it through supplements and food—preferably food since our body can absorb it better.

Milk and dairy products are the most popular source for calcium, but don't forget about naturally occurring calcium in other foods. All of these items are excellent sources of calcium to consider for your no-cook food storage:

- Seeds: chia, poppy, sunflower, and sesame
- Sardines and canned salmon (with bones)
- Beans and lentils
- Almonds
- Whey protein
- Leafy greens
- Figs
- Blackstrap molasses

It's also a good idea to add a calcium supplement to your food storage. And remember, the body needs vitamin D to absorb calcium. We get vitamin D from sunlight (although it's difficult to get enough D from the sun in the Northern Hemisphere, especially during the winter months), our diet (mainly meats and fish), and supplements. Consult your medical provider for the best supplements for you and your family.

It's also important to note that, while many foods are excellent sources of calcium, some foods block calcium absorption. And some, like beans and leafy greens, are both a great source of calcium *and* a calcium blocker. Phytates, or phytic acid, is a natural substance found in plant seeds. It occurs naturally in all grains, legumes, nuts, and seeds. When the seeds sprout, the phytate is broken down.

Beans, which are high in calcium, are often cooked without proper preparation to release the phytic acid. Grains, such as wheat, are usually processed whole (milled) without the seed sprouting and made into a slice of bread to have alongside your bowl of beans. The phytic acid in the grain is left intact. The phytates then bind with minerals like calcium and block the bodies absorption. So, your calcium-rich bowl of beans and slice of bread are in a form your body can't use.

Let's say you add a lovely raw spinach salad alongside your beans and bread. A cup of raw spinach has approximately 30 milligrams of calcium—a small dent in the recommended 1,000 milligrams per day. But hey, it's something. Or is it?

In addition to being a source of calcium, spinach is also high in oxalic acid. Like the phytates in grains, legumes, nuts, and seeds, the oxalic acid found in leafy greens impedes the absorption of calcium by binding with the mineral.

You can schedule your meals to not eat calcium-binding foods at the same time as calcium-rich foods. Or you can learn a few tricks that will reduce the phytates in grains, legumes, nuts, and seeds while turning them into wonderful no-cook or low-cook foods and nutritional powerhouses. We'll learn more in the following chapters.

Note: Dehydrating cheese at home is not recommended because of the high fat content, which can cause rancidity and prevent the cheese from being shelf stable. If you do choose to dehydrate cheese at home, it should be stored in the freezer. Extra-hard cheeses, like Parmesan, do better dehydrated and kept for a limited time. You can safely use a home freeze dryer for long-term cheese storage. Purchasing freeze-dried cheese and butter from a commercial retailer is also an option.

Cooler Yogurt

While this truly is very cool yogurt, I call it Cooler Yogurt because of the method used. No need for a fancy yogurt maker when you have a cooler, mason jars, boiling water, and a few towels! This can be made from any type of milk. Raw or pasteurized cow or goat milk are wonderful, but powdered milk works too. I prefer full-fat powdered milk, but you can make it from nonfat, too, if that's how you roll.

You'll need a starter culture. I keep a few options on hand: yogurt purchased from the grocery store that says "contains live cultures" on the container, dehydrated yogurt bark—made from yogurt that had active cultures and is rehydrated before use, and commercially purchased freeze-dried yogurt starter cultures (I store these in the freezer).

If using a commercial freeze-dried starter culture, this may only make one quart of yogurt (read instructions included with your culture). Once you have this one quart, use it as your starter for this recipe.

When making yogurt, or any culture or ferment, it's important to start with very clean equipment. Wash your pot, thermometer, jars, ladle, and funnel.

Equipment Needed:

- Heavy-bottomed large pot (Dutch oven or stock pot)
- Thermometer (important)
- Medium-sized cooler
- One or two bath towels (for inside the cooler)
- Another towel or two, or a blanket (for on top of the cooler)
- 4 quart-size canning jars with lids + 1 pint jar with a lid
- A 5th quart-size lidded jar or an additional pint jar (for hot water)
- Ladle
- Food funnel
- Fork

Ingredients:

- 1 gallon of milk (if using dry milk powder, reconstitute according to package instructions, whisking well so there are no lumps)
- ½ cup plain yogurt starter (fully hydrated yogurt)

Pour the milk into the pot. Heat over low to medium-low, watching and stirring regularly, until it reaches 180°. Remove from heat.

With the lid on, let the milk cool down to 115°. This may take a few hours. I set an alarm to check the temperature every half hour at first and more often as it gets close to 115°. You can cool it quicker by putting the pot in a sink of cold water. Pay very close attention to the thermometer; 115° is key.

When the temperature is close to 115 (say around 125°) prepare your cooler/incubator. Lay a folded towel across the bottom of the cooler. You want it to lay flat so the jars (all five) will sit solidly. Take your fifth quart jar or additional pint jar and add hot water (from the tap or heated on the stove to around 120°). Put the lid on the jar and place in the cooler. This will keep your cooler warm while the yogurt is in it.

When your milk has reached 115°, prepare your starter culture. Place your starter in a glass measuring cup. Add a few tablespoons of the warm milk to the culture and stir. Add more milk, a tablespoon at a time, until the yogurt is brought up to the milk temperature (or close to, no need to test) and has a thick, gravy-like consistency.

With your incubator ready, the culture ready, and the milk at 115°, it's time to prepare the yogurt. Using the food funnel, ladle the warm milk into the quart jars and the pint, leaving and inch to an inch and a half space at the top. Divvy up the pourable yogurt between the jars; you won't need as much in the pint as you use in the quarts. Mix well with a clean fork. Put the lids on, tightening slightly.

Place the jars in the cooler with the hot water jar. Tuck a towel over the top of the jars, then close the lid. Tuck another towel or blanket over the cooler. Allow it to sit undisturbed for at least 8 hours and up to 24. For incubations over 12 hours, refresh the water every 12 hours so it stays hot. The longer the yogurt incubates, the more tart it will be because the sugars are reduced with long incubations. Twelve hours is about perfect for my husband and son, but I like a longer incubation.

When finished incubating, move the jars of yogurt to the refrigerator (or another cold location) and allow to chill. Plain yogurt can be flavored just about any way you wish! Fruit powders, jams, and fresh, dried, or canned fruit are excellent. The options are endless. Plain yogurt also makes a nice salad dressing base when combined with mayonnaise.

Nuts and Nut Butters

Nuts and nut butters are a great addition for short-term food storage but don't have the stability of keeping for years and years. The natural oils in nuts can cause rancidity. That said, with proper packaging and storing in a cool, dry environment, you can get a year or two of freshness, or maybe even longer.

In this chapter, we'll discuss a variety of nuts—or what is commonly referred to as nuts. Peanuts are actually a legume (like a bean), and cashews are really seeds. For our purposes, they're under the "nut" umbrella.

Nuts still in the shell will stay fresh longer, but not all varieties are available this way. Sometimes, around the holidays I'll see walnuts, hazelnuts, and other nuts in the shell, but the cost is usually at a premium. Cashews are never sold in the shell because of allergy issues. The shell contains chemicals similar to poison ivy. For this same reason, cashews may be labeled as raw, but they have been heat treated to remove any dangerous substances.

Almonds are another nut often advertised as raw that are not truly raw. In 2007, the USDA passed a mandatory program for almond pasteurization after cases of salmonella were traced back to raw almonds. There are two common almond pasteurization methods: "washing" the almonds with steam or fumigation of the almonds with propylene oxide gas. I look for steam-pasteurized almonds for my pantry.

One main reason I look for raw nuts is because they can be soaked and sprouted to improve digestibility. Even though they may be referred to as nut sprouts, they are really more of a soak since the process is stopped before the tails are formed. Beginning with a raw nut or peanut, giving it a soak, then rinsing for a day or two, followed by dehydrating, results in wonderful and delicious crispy nuts. Or you can skip the dehydrating and eat the soaks raw.

Nuts do swell somewhat during the sprouting (soaking) process. Depending on the nut, your yield may be 1.25:1 up to 2:1. So you could start with 1 cup of nuts and end up with 1¼ cups or even 2 cups. I'll be honest, while I've read about yields of 2:1, I've never achieved it; 1.5:1 is more realistic. Even so, it's a great way to increase the volume while also making them easier on the gut, which is important if you're eating a lot of nuts.

We buy raw nuts in bulk to vacuum seal, then store them in a cool, dark location. We also have some walnuts, from my husband's grandma's walnut tree, that we've kept in the freezer for a few years now. They are still surprisingly fresh!

Even though most of our nut storage is "raw" almonds, we add in containers of roasted peanuts or mixes when we find a good deal on them. If these are purchased in plastic jars with a lid and a seal under the lid, I leave them as is for storage. If they are in those cardboard-style cans, they need to be vacuum sealed for maximum storage time.

I also like the little fancy cans of flavored nuts. Ounce per ounce, they are terribly expensive, but it takes only a small amount of them in the form of a garnish to really add flavor to a dish. When I find a good sale, I buy several cans. These are also vacuum sealed, labeled with the variety/flavor, and dated.

The ease of just opening up a jar or vacuum bag and having quick and easy nutrition makes nuts a winner for me in our no-cook food storage. By regularly rotating nuts (eat what you store) and following FIFO, you can ensure a fresh product. By being realistic and storing the quantity of nuts you use in your everyday life within a year or two, you'll prevent waste.

In addition to whole nuts (or nut pieces), nut butters play a substantial roll in our pantry. Peanut butter is a mainstay in our everyday life, not only for sandwiches but as a component for fruit dip, dressings, sauces, and more. As my growing son has a harder time filling his belly, we've upped our peanut butter storage to accommodate for quick meals and snacks. We also have peanut butter in our get-home bags, keeping a small jar and a spoon at the ready. Perfect no-cook food storage!

Commercial peanut or almond butter has a shelf life of about 18 months past the best-by date when unopened. I've had a jar just under three years past the best-by date and it was fine, but the storage was probably perfect—a cool, dark closet.

If you buy natural peanut butter, without preservatives, these may have a shorter shelf life. Again, use the best-by date as a guide but expect another six months or so depending on how you store it.

This is also the perfect place to mention seed butters, such as sunflower seed or sesame seed (usually called tahini). These items are worth considering for your food storage if they have a place in your daily life.

Another excellent item to consider for your no-cook food storage is peanut butter powder. The peanuts are roasted and then pressed to remove excess oil before being ground into a powder. The now-defatted peanut butter powder is lower in fat and calories.

I purchased my first jar of peanut butter powder by mistake, not truly realizing what it was on a rush-through-the-store grocery trip. When I got it home and realized my mistake, I was going to return it but never did. When making smoothies one morning before leaving to go skiing, I decided to use the peanut butter powder instead of opening a new jar of regular peanut butter. I've been a fan ever since!

The lower in calories part of the peanut butter powder appeals to me and my middle-aged waistline. We add it to smoothies or sprinkle it over oatmeal. Because it's a powder, it blends in easily, which also makes it excellent for dressings and sauces.

The lower-calorie aspect is perfect for me now. But in a long-term food emergency, restricting calories may not be necessary, so you'll want to add fat back to the peanut butter powder. Check out my recipe for Peanut Dressing or Sauce for a creamy and delicious plant-based protein option using traditional fats.

Even though it's been defatted, I haven't found longer best-by dates on the powder compared to regular peanut butter. But, like the peanut butter, I'm using them well past the stamped dates without issue. Use your judgment.

Although I only have peanut butter powder as part of my larder, you can also find almond butter powder, cashew powder, and I'm sure other nut options. There's even sunflower seed powder for those who are nut-free.

Peanut Dressing or Sauce

This dressing is pure peanuty deliciousness! It has just a bit of sweet and just a bit of spice, making the perfect combination. I used to make a different version of this dressing with the blender. This one is an adaptation of that recipe (I've been making it for so long I've lost the original) and Asian Peanut Dressing from *The Ridiculously Big Salad* by Amanda Rose, PhD.

Use it on greens as a great way to up their calorie count, as a dip for veggie sticks, and even as a sauce for chicken or pasta. Using peanut butter powder allows it to blend super smoothly with a whisk in seconds. The peanut butter option takes a few more strokes but still works fine.

This recipe makes enough dressing for four average-size salads. Each serving will give about 400 calories with 35 grams of fat, 17 grams of protein, and 8 grams of carbohydrates. Or make as written for the Rice Noodles with Peanut Sauce recipe found in the Noodles and Flakes section.

- ½ cup olive oil, avocado oil, or a combination of the two
- 2 tablespoons sesame oil or toasted sesame oil
- ½ cup peanut butter powder
- 1 teaspoon powdered ginger
- ½ teaspoon garlic powder
- 2 teaspoons dried coriander flakes or parsley flakes
- Pinch of red pepper flakes and/or a dash of Sriracha sauce (or more, depending on how hot you like it)
- ⅓ cup apple cider vinegar
- ⅓ cup soy sauce or tamari
- Sea salt, to taste
- Ground black pepper, to taste
- Sweetener of choice, to taste (you won't need much, if any)
- Water for thinning (optional)

In a medium bowl or a 4-cup measuring cup, add the oils and peanut butter powder. Whisk until smooth. Add the spices and herbs, then whisk again. Add the vinegar and soy sauce, stirring carefully to combine. Give it a taste before adding salt, pepper, and optional sweetener.

If you're using this as a salad dressing, veggie dip, or sauce for meat, it is probably the correct consistency. If you're using it as a pasta sauce, it may need thinning. The reserved cooking water from your pasta is perfect for this. Combine the pasta with the sauce, then add a tablespoon of water at a time until it's the consistency you want.

Variation:

Substitute ¼ cup peanut butter for the peanut butter powder (use ⅓ cup if you like a more peanuty taste). If you use ⅓ cup of peanut butter, reduce the olive oil to ⅓ cup also. The rest of the ingredients remain the same.

Put the peanut butter in a medium bowl or a 4-cup measuring cup (I like to use measuring cups for easy pouring). Add a little of the oil and whisk to combine. Keep adding the oil a little at a time until the peanut butter thins and is easy to stir. Then proceed with the remaining ingredients in order, following the original directions.

No-Cook Choco-Peanut-Coconut Fat Bomb

These high-fat, bite-sized snacks are a great quick treat. Each ball is approximately 110 calories, 9 grams of fat, and 2.5 grams of protein. If using 1 tablespoon of honey as the sweetener, the carb count is around 5. Stevia drops the carbs to about 3.5.

- 4 tablespoons peanut butter
- 2 tablespoons peanut butter powder
- 2 tablespoons unsweetened cocoa powder
- 2 tablespoons coconut oil, refined or unrefined
- ¾ cup unsweetened shredded coconut
- 1 teaspoon vanilla extract
- Honey, maple syrup, or liquid stevia, to taste
- 2 tablespoons water, divided (optional)

In a medium bowl, combine all ingredients except sweetener and water. Once mixed, add the sweetener to taste. If using honey or maple syrup, start with ½ tablespoon and add more if desired. Because of the liquid in these sweeteners, you may not need the optional water. If using stevia, add a few drops until it's the correct sweetness. Add water, 1 teaspoon at a time, until a soft dough forms.

Once the dough is perfectly sweetened, use a teaspoon or small cookie scoop to create walnut-sized balls. These hold up okay at room temperature as long as it isn't too hot. Remember, coconut oil is liquid above 77° Fahrenheit.

Seeds

There's a huge variety of seeds to consider for your no-cook food storage. Not only seeds for your garden, sometimes referred to in preparedness circles as a seed vault, but seeds ready to eat with minimal preparation.

Let's talk about garden seeds first. Lettuce and radishes go from seed to edible in a matter of weeks and make a lovely, fresh food. Tomatoes are the most commonly grown garden item. Cucumber and zucchini are also popular among home growers.

As mentioned earlier, the calorie count of all of these is low, less than 10 calories per cup of lettuce, only around 1 calorie in each single radish, 39 calories in ½ cup of tomatoes, and 8 and 10 calories in ½ cup of cucumbers and zucchini, respectively.

With these low numbers, it's nearly impossible to meet your daily caloric needs with these popular garden items. The addition of calorie-laden dressings will go a long way in adding to the calorie count. Remember, 1 tablespoon of olive oil adds 120 calories. Vinaigrette anyone?

A cup of kale comes in higher than lettuce at 33 calories per cup. While lettuce is wonderful eaten raw, kale, spinach, and other heavy leafy greens are best cooked due to their goitrogenic compounds that increase the need for iodine. If these heavy greens are consumed raw in large amounts, they can affect thyroid function. While raw is fine on occasion, it's best not to eat these heavy greens daily without cooking them.

Garden vegetables higher in calories include shell beans grown for the bean inside (pinto, navy, etc.), potatoes, corn, green peas, and sweet potato. Fruits like grapes and blueberries also come in at a higher calorie count than kale. Calorie density is certainly something to consider when planning your seed vault.

Another thing to consider is the gardening process. I found a love for gardening in my early twenties. I was a mom to two young girls then, and the three of us had a raised garden bed on the end of the house. We spent almost every evening tending our little garden and playing outside.

A few other women in the neighborhood and their children would often stop by, and the kids could do their thing while I chatted with the moms and worked on my weeding. I did vertical gardening then, with cucumber vines growing up the side of my house, shading the windows. I'll admit, I was rather full of myself and considered myself an amazing gardener.

That consideration of my gardening prowess continued until 2009, the year I moved to Central Wyoming. Growing a garden in Wyoming was nothing like growing a garden in the Pacific Northwest! The soil is sandy. The weather is dry. And then there's wind. Lots and lots of wind, sucking the moisture right out of my poor plants. There were rabbits and deer waiting for me to turn my back and snack on my hard-toiled, sad-looking plants.

It got even worse in 2010, when my newly planted trees and struggling garden were wiped out in hours by a hoard of grasshoppers. I'd never seen anything like it.

For the past six years, I've lived in Northern Wyoming. I still struggle to produce anything resembling a decent garden. We planted bushes and trees, too, in hopes of creating a food forest. While some are doing well, we've yet to harvest any fruit or nuts. Sadly, we planted them during drought years, which may have stunted their growth.

This year, with a decent amount of rain and a higher water table, they do seem to be perking up, so maybe next year we'll have fruit. The vegetable garden is plugging along, with one beautiful tomato plant (32 calories per cup of raw tomatoes, 39 calories per half cup cooked), several others looking okay, and the promise of lots of summer squash. A few days ago, the chickens and a wild rabbit got in the garden and snacked on the cabbage.

With a growing season of 111 days, we do what we can to grow during this time. We extend our greens harvest by planting them early, in boxes covered with shower doors to bring in extra heat. We use the same method for a fall salad box and have harvested greens into December. A greenhouse would also be a good idea and is on our list.

Last year, my neighbor got a beautiful new greenhouse. I told my husband, "This is exactly what I want. If it survives the winter winds, I'm getting one in the spring." Sadly, a huge windstorm—the biggest we've had since we moved here—swept through in the middle of November and destroyed her greenhouse. I'm back to shopping for one sturdy enough to withstand our record-setting winds.

All of this to say . . . if you have seeds stored to use for an emergency but you don't garden, you may want to rethink this. It's possible you'll have the same success I did for twenty years in the Pacific Northwest. However, it's likely you may have my Wyoming experience. The soil may not be what you need for a successful garden without being amended.

Do you have a fence that will keep out pests? Do you have enough seeds—and the right varieties—to provide the calories you need? And what about next year? Do you have the skills and knowledge to save your garden seeds? Speaking about what types of seeds are best to store in your seed vault, are they heirloom seeds suitable for saving year after year while remaining true to what they should be?

These are things I'd recommend studying and learning. With the proper knowledge and supplies, you may be able to grow many, many things. But learning what you need now will benefit you if you're ever in an emergency situation and relying on what you have on hand.

Note: This seems like a good place to mention foraging for food. There're many wild edibles and medicinals available worldwide. Learning what's in your area or region is a smart idea. Being able to identify these wild items is imperative before determining if they're safe to eat. I'm sure we've all heard the advice that every mushroom is edible . . . once. The moral: If you eat it, it could kill you.

While foraging is something I'm interested in and studying, I am not qualified to teach on it or even really offer advice. Find a qualified source to learn from to add this important skill and knowledge to your repertoire.

Now that the whole garden and foraging talk is out of the way, let's talk about the other seeds I keep in my no-cook food storage.

Seeds for Sprouting

I sprout a variety of small seeds: radish, alfalfa, clover, and much more. These small seeds grow into beautiful long sprouts over about a week. After the first few days, we give them indirect sunlight so they can green up. At still only about 10 calories a cup, they're not going to give you the energy needed for a day of gardening in the hot sun. They do, however, taste amazing.

They also grow year-round.

During the long, dark days of winter, fresh sprouts offer a taste of spring. I love the bite of a sprinkle of radish sprouts added to a simple winter salad of stored shredded carrots and stored chopped apples. Again, the addition of a fatty dressing will up the calorie count.

My favorite source for sprouting seeds is Sprout People. They're more expensive than other places, but they have a huge selection, and The University of California Publication 8151 recommends Sprout People as a safe seed source.

Commercial sprouts have been linked to outbreaks of salmonella and E. coli. Alfalfa, radish, and mung bean have frequently been found as the source of these outbreaks, but all raw sprouts pose a risk. Using quality seeds, clean equipment, and safe practices are important. Please refer to "California Publication 8151" and "Sprouting Seeds at Home Safely, Extension Food Safety Fact Sheet–July 2018," both listed in the Resources, for more information on safe practices.

Seeds for sprouting store well and remain fresh for a at least a year when vacuum sealed (some sources say up to five years). Sealing in small packages makes the most sense for me. I like bags of about 6 tablespoons, which is enough for three or four sprouting sessions, depending on my sprouting device.

For small seeds, I use a mason jar with a sprout lid, an Easy Sprouter (a low-water use brand name device), or a vertical sprouter. For in-depth information on seed sprouting, check out my book *Sprouts for Your Food Storage*.

You can also let your sprouts grow out to become microgreens. Sprouting wheat, spelt, farrow, or einkorn takes several days to develop tails and, when finished, still tend to be a little too al dente to eat raw. However, growing out these cereal grains into microgreens gives them the ability to become no-cook food. Microgreens take about two weeks until they're ready to eat.

Chia Seeds

These powerful little gems have a mild flavor, tending to take on the flavor of whatever they're mixed with. When added to water or other liquid, they plump up into a gelatinous pudding-like dish. I'm not overly fond of chia seeds because they stick in my teeth, but their nutritional profile is hard to beat.

Chia seeds are loaded with fiber, protein, omega-3 fatty acids, and various micronutrients. Two tablespoons of chia seeds contain 138 calories and 14 percent of the recommended daily value of calcium. And yes, they are the same seeds that are loved for growing "hair" on Chia Pets, making them also suitable as a microgreen.

Chia seeds can be eaten raw, soaked in water or juice, sprinkled on oatmeal or yogurt, made into a pudding, added to smoothies, and so much more.

When added to water, chia seeds become gelatinous. Because of this, chia (along with flaxseed) is widely used as an egg substitute. Simply grind the chia seeds into a fine, flakey powder and add water, then let set for five minutes. Use 1 tablespoon of ground chia plus 3 tablespoons of water for each egg needed.

Chia or flaxseed "eggs" can be used in baked goods such as cakes, quick breads, or muffins. They don't work well for cookies but are excellent for cookie bars. Chia or flaxseed eggs are not recommended for pancakes since the inside remains gummy and the outside burns before the pancakes can cook through.

Some sources indicate chia seeds can last up to five years when properly packaged and stored (cool, low-light locations). Because of the fat in chia seeds, they can go rancid. You'll know by the smell. I use my vacuum sealer to store chia seeds, making small packages that can be used up within a few weeks once opened.

Flaxseed

Like chia, flaxseed also has some excellent health benefits, including providing a good amount of protein, fiber, omega-3 fatty acids, vitamins, and minerals. It's a little lighter in calories at 74 per 2 tablespoons.

Being high in fiber, flaxseed is an excellent addition to your no-cook food storage. Any change in diet can disrupt the digestive system and cause irregularity. Adding ground flaxseed can help combat this. Flaxseed oil, mentioned in the Traditional Fats chapter, works in the same way and is excellent when drizzled on a salad or added to a smoothie.

Flaxseed should be stored whole but ground before consumption for maximum digestion. Left whole, it could pass through your system without giving you the benefits it provides. I like to use a small, manual coffee grinder for small seeds like flax. Once ground, sprinkle over oatmeal or yogurt, or add to smoothies or baked goods. Like chia, flaxseed is an egg substitute.

Flaxseed can become rancid. The best-by date on flaxseed is usually somewhere between one and two years. Like everything, proper storage can extend this. Vacuum sealing it in small quantities is my preferred storage method.

Poppy Seeds

High in fiber and plant-based fats, the nutritional profile of poppy seeds may surprise you. Two tablespoons provide 96 calories and 7.4 grams of fat! Keep in mind, fat helps you feel full and satiated, making these little seeds a smart choice for your no-cook food storage. They're also high in calcium, giving somewhere between 4 and 10 percent of your recommended daily value per single tablespoon!

Poppy seeds can be left whole and sprinkled over oatmeal or yogurt, or added to smoothies and baked goods. Poppy Seed Dressing is one of my favorite ways to add poppy seeds to my no-cook repertoire. Check the Resources section for a link to my current favorite version of this dressing.

The high oil content of poppy seeds can lead to rancidity. Even so, when properly stored, you should be able to get a few years out of them. Practice FIFO and package in small, vacuum-sealed containers.

Sesame Seeds

Another excellent source of plant-based protein, fat, and fiber are sesame seeds. They can be sprinkled into other no-cook or low-cook foods. Sesame seeds are the perfect addition to a sushi roll, like the one I share later in this chapter. Sesame seeds are also an excellent add in for Nut and Fruit Balls, shared in the Commercially Preserved chapter.

Sunflower, Pumpkin, and Other Miscellaneous Seeds

The variety of seeds you may wish to add to your no-cook food storage is almost endless! Because of their oily nature, you'll want to use the same storage methods mentioned in previous sections—low light, cool temps, and vacuum packaging in quantities you can use in a reasonable time after opening.

Vanilla Chia Pudding

This recipe makes a single serving. Scale up as needed. I use a glass bowl with a lid or a ½-pint mason jar with a lid when making the single serving size. This is a great breakfast, snack, or dessert. One serving, using whole cow milk and honey, is approximately 183 calories with 8 grams each of fat and protein.

- ½ cup milk, dairy or nondairy (reconstituted if using from powder)
- 2 tablespoons chia seeds
- 1 teaspoon honey (or use a low-carb sweetener such as monk fruit or stevia)
- ½ teaspoon vanilla extract

Combine all ingredients in a bowl or mason jar. Mix well. Add the lid and put in the fridge (or other cold area) for at least three hours, preferably overnight.

When ready to serve, dress it up with toppings as desired, such as fruit (fresh, dried, or canned), shredded coconut, jam or preserves, chopped nuts, etc. You could add a teaspoon or so of peanut butter powder to increase the protein by a few grams.

Tuna Rolls

My son loves all things Japanese, including sushi! We make a variety of sushi-like rolls at home. This simple Tuna Roll was included in my *Sprouts for Your Food Storage* book. I wanted to offer it here, as written, plus give some ideas on how this can be a no-cook or low-cook meal.

Sushi rolls are basically a variation of a sandwich. The nori is the bread or wrapper. In Japanese culture, they have the onigirazu, which originated from a comic book in the '90s. Rice is spread on nori, then piled high with rice ball (onigiri or omusubi) fillings.

Popular fillings include salted salmon, tuna with mayo, ham and egg, chicken in mayo, shrimp tempura, and/or assorted vegetables. But an onigirazu doesn't always have these traditional fillings. It can also have sandwich-style fillings, and instead of being rolled with a bamboo mat, the onigirazu is folded to create a square-shaped parcel to hold in the fillings.

We like nori not only for the slightly fishy flavor but because it's a good source of iodine. If you're a nori fan, give regular rolls, onigirazu, or handrolls a try and see if this concept works for your no-cook food storage.

Handrolls are the easiest of all. The sheet of nori is cut in half, the fillings are added, and then it's rolled like an ice cream cone. Where regular rolls and onigirazu rely on the sticky rice to hold everything together, handrolls don't need to hold together in the same way.

This simple Tuna Roll makes a delicious lunch and is one of our favorites. It's also a great use of leftover rice. Cold-soaked rice, described in the Noodles and Flakes chapter, could be used.

Add extra water when soaking, and let it go longer than you think is necessary so it's as sticky as possible. You may need to drain off excess water. Or, skip the additional water but do stir in a little rice wine vinegar and a sprinkle of sweetener. It should hold together fairly well, but it won't be professional sushi roll quality. The onigirazu or handroll should work great.

I list tuna with mayo (check out my homemade mayo in the Herbs, Spices, Sweeteners, and Sauces chapter) as the filling in this recipe, but the sky is truly the limit. If you're a sardine fan, they are amazing inside a roll. Choose your veggies based on what is available.

- 1 cup cooked rice (white, brown, jasmine, basmati, etc.)
- ½ cup water, divided
- 1½ tablespoons rice wine vinegar
- Sprinkle of sugar (optional; I use a less-processed sugar like Sucanat)
- 1 can Albacore tuna, drained
- 1 to 2 tablespoons mayonnaise
- Sprinkle of garlic powder

- ½ ripe avocado, thinly sliced
- 1 carrot, grated
- ½ cucumber, seeded and cut in strips (optional)
- ¼ bell pepper, cut lengthwise in thin strips (optional; red is beautiful but green tastes just as good)
- 3 cups alfalfa, radish, clover, or other "green" sprouts
- 3 nori sheets

To make the pseudo sushi rice, reheat cooked rice with ¼ cup of the water. Cover but keep an eye on it so it doesn't stick. After a few minutes, give it a stir. Add the remaining ¼ cup of water, rice wine vinegar, and a sprinkle of sugar. Stir and heat through. Your rice should be somewhat sticky. Set aside and let cool slightly.

In a small bowl, combine tuna, mayo, and garlic powder. Mix well. I like the tuna to be fairly broken up and somewhat smooth.

Lay one sheet of nori on a bamboo mat, shiny side down.

Put ⅓ of the rice on the nori and spread gently with the back of a spoon. You want to cover to the edges and flatten the rice, but don't smash it. Make sure the far side of the nori (the edge farthest from you) has rice on it. The rice will "seal" the roll.

Add ⅓ of the prepared tuna in a line about an inch or so from the edge of the nori nearest you. Add ⅓ of the avocado, grated carrot, cucumber, and bell pepper. Top with 1 cup of sprouts.

Beginning on the edge closest to you, roll tightly, making sure to "tuck" the fillings as you go. Move to a cutting board.

Roll the remaining two.

Use a sharp knife to cut the roll. I cut in half and then cut each half in thirds.

Variation: Spicy Tuna Roll

Add a squirt of Sriracha Sauce to the mayonnaise when mixing the tuna. Proceed with recipe as written.

I like to make a Sriracha Mayo Sauce for dipping too. Combine ¼ cup mayo with a few squirts of Sriracha (how hot do you like it?!) and a drop or two of soy sauce. Mix well. You can dip your cut pieces of sushi in the sauce or spread more sauce on top of each piece.

Pseudo Sushi Rice

Reheat cooked rice with ¼ cup of the water. Cover it but keep an eye on it so it doesn't stick. After a few minutes, give it a stir. Add the remaining ¼ cup of water, rice wine vinegar, and sprinkle of sugar. Stir and heat through. Your rice should be somewhat sticky. Set aside and let cool slightly.

Wrapper Alternatives

There are a few no-cook or low-cook alternatives to nori. Rice paper, or spring roll wrappers, are very thin sheets of pressed rice and have a wonderfully long shelf life. They are stiff but become pliable when set in warm water for only a few seconds. Use them like you would a burrito, filling with just about anything you have on hand and rolling up. The rice paper is translucent, so you'll even get to see your food through it.

Lettuce or cabbage are other popular wrappers. If you're growing these in your garden, take advantage and load them with sandwich fillings.

You may want to consider homemade tortillas, crepes, or flatbread. While not no-cook, these are low-cook items made on a stovetop. They do have some aroma when cooking, so they may not be a good option for a densely populated area. But if you're cooking inside with the windows closed, the odors should be minimal.

You'll find recipes for sourdough tortillas and flatbread in my book *Sourdough for Your Food Storage*. Erin's Sourdough Crepes, linked in the Resources section, are excellent. Substitute powdered eggs, coconut or olive oil, and stored milk for the fresh ingredients—they'll still taste good.

Legumes: Beans and Pulses

While often used interchangeably, there is a difference between legumes, beans, and pulses. According to Harvard T.H. Chan School of Public Health, a legume refers to any plant from the Fabaceae family that would include its leaves, stems, and pods. A pulse is the edible seed from a legume plant. Pulses include beans, lentils, and peas. For example, a pea pod is a legume, but the pea inside the pod is the pulse (source 1).

Peanuts, because they grow in pods, are a legume but not a bean or pulse. They're also not a nut, but for the purposes of this book, they're discussed in the section Nuts and Nut Butters. In this chapter, we are going to focus on dried pulses, which include those commonly referred to as beans, peas, or lentils.

With proper packaging (mylar bags with oxygen absorbers, stored in a sealed bucket), pulses will keep for up to 30 years and are one of the most popular food storage items. These pulses—which, for the sake of convenience, I'll refer to as beans going forward—are relatively inexpensive, making them economical for bulk purchases.

I recently ordered an assortment of beans in 25-pound bags from Azure Standard. Depending on the variety, I paid between 91¢ and $1.96 per pound for organically grown items, with whole peas being the least expensive and mung beans the most. In my local chain grocery store, a pound of nonorganic beans starts around 88¢ for pinto beans in five-pound bags.

Bean nutrition varies slightly based on variety, but overall, they're considered an excellent source of plant-based protein, high in fiber while low in fat, and high in a wide variety of vitamins and minerals, including calcium. Beans are an excellent source of folate, the natural form of B9, which is essential during a time of rapid growth such as pregnancy.

Beans do have a bit of a reputation as being hard to digest and producing unseemly side effects. Have you heard the little ditty about beans being the magical fruit? Beans are also well-known for needing to cook for an extended about of time to make them palatable. You may be wondering why I have an entire section dedicated to them in a *no-cook* cookbook!

What if I told you that, by sprouting, you could drastically cut down or even eliminate the need for cooking? It's true!

Hard beans, like pinto, black, and white, will benefit from cooking even after sprouting. Alternatively, mung, garbanzo, whole or split peas, and lentils can be eaten raw after a long soak and several days of sprouting. An added benefit to sprouting is the improvement of digestion, making beans much more gut friendly and cutting down—or even eliminating—embarrassing side effects.

Sprouting requires little fancy equipment. When sprouting beans, I usually use a pot or bowl for soaking and a kitchen colander or strainer for sprouting.

Sprouting Beans

Soak your beans for at least 12 hours and up to 24 hours, changing the water about halfway through.

Drain the beans into a colander and give them a good rinse in cool water.

Shake, tip, tilt, and move that colander to remove as much water as possible. I spend a couple of minutes doing this at the sink.

Set the colander on an out-of-the-way counter with a dish underneath to catch any drips, and cover with a kitchen towel.

Twelve hours later, repeat the process.

Now taste your bean (do not taste kidney beans; see note at the end of this chapter). It should be softish. You probably won't see a tail (sprout) yet, but you may see a bulge at the germ end of some of the beans.

At each rinsing, you want to taste your bean so you can develop an idea of how you want your beans to taste when eating raw. I've found beans to have a fresh, sometimes grassy flavor. I'll admit, this isn't popular with everyone. But the more often you eat beans raw, the better they'll taste to you. Exposure helps us like certain foods. There is some evidence that suggests, at least for children, introducing a food a dozen times is the key.

After tasting, move your colander of beans back to their spot on the counter and cover again. Every 12 hours, you'll shake, rinse, and taste the beans until you determine they are finished sprouting. Usually, this takes only two to four days, but time may vary based on weather. Sprouting happens quicker in hot weather and takes longer when it's cold. Speaking of hot weather, if it's extremely hot and humid, consider rinsing your beans three times a day.

The recommendation for sprouting mung beans is slightly different. You'll still use a colander as your sprouting vehicle, but add a weight to the top of the beans in the colander, such as a heavy plate. Leave the plate in place and continuing rinsing every 8 to 12 hours. The weight of the plate allows them to grow fatter and straighter.

Keeping mung beans covered and preventing sunlight also stops them from greening. Sunlight will cause your mung beans to have green sections or leaves. I've made more than one batch of less-than-attractive mung beans. Beans that were too skinny. Too crooked. And even with funny green wings. They still tasted good and worked well for my needs. If you'd like better-looking beans, check the Resources section for more detailed instructions.

While these are very simple directions for sprouting beans and will work wonderfully, you could certainly explore other sprouting devices and methods, plus learn how to sprout other food storage items. In my book *Sprouts for Your Food Storage*, I detail how to sprout seeds, legumes, and grains, plus how to soak nuts for digestion. I also share my favorite sprouting devices, which include the colander, mason jars with sprout lids, and a few low-water sprouting containers for times when water is scarce.

Sprouts have such a place in our lives, we often take a pound of lentils with us on multiday backpacking or camping trips! It's a great way to have something fresh after several days in the wild.

Keep reading for my Marinated Lentils recipe, one of my favorite ways to enjoy raw sprouted lentils. Because of the phytic acid in legumes, raw is not recommended by the Weston A. Price Foundation. Here's an excerpt from the article "Living with Phytic Acid": *"But raw is definitely not Nature's way for grains, nuts, seeds and beans. . . and even some tubers, like yams; nor are quick cooking or rapid heat processes like extrusion."*

While eating raw beans is not recommended, the sprouting process opens up the seed and reduces the phytase, making them more digestible and reducing the mineral absorption issues. To increase the digestibility and absorption, you can steam lentils, garbanzo beans, or peas for a few minutes. They'll still hold their shape and are perfect to use in salads. Lightly steamed garbanzo beans are wonderful mashed into a hummus style dip. Mung beans are very popular for use in a stir-fry.

Though not recommended by WAPF, I am comfortable eating sprouted lentils, peas, and mung beans raw along with mashing raw sprouted garbanzo and other beans. Once sprouted, I find the digestibility issues are eliminated and believe the phytase is adequately reduced. You'll want to make your own decision about raw versus steamed or cooked for these types of pulses.

Hard beans, like pinto, white, or black, benefit from cooking until fully soft after sprouting. This releases the sugars and gives them a better taste. Because you took the time to sprout, they'll cook quickly. A Sun Oven, Wonder Oven, or hay box is a great way to cook beans. During the winter months, I cook them on my woodstove. I have more information on these cooking processes in the section Fuel-Saving and Low-Odor Cooking Methods later in this book.

Note: A special and important note about kidney beans—raw kidney beans contain very high amounts of phytohemagglutinin, which can lead to food poisoning, including symptoms such as nausea, vomiting, and diarrhea. I rarely sprout kidney beans. When I do, I <u>do not</u> taste them during the sprouting process. I judge the beans' readiness by sight only. When I determine they've sprouted long enough, I bring them to a rolling boil for 10 minutes. (This is the minimum for safety; some sources recommend 30 minutes at a hard boil.) Drain off the cooking water, then you can finish cooking them in fresh water, using your choice of cooking method such as stovetop, crockpot, Instant Pot, etc.

Sprouting is a wonderful way to have no-cook or low-cook beans. But for those who prefer their dry beans cooked slowly until creamy, and without little sprout tails, there are low fuel ways of doing this. Be sure to visit the Fuel-Saving and Low-Odor Cooking Methods chapter.

Another great use for beans, especially older beans that may not have been properly packaged for long-term storage, is to grind them into a flour or meal. More on this in the chapter Flours and Meals.

Marinated Lentils

These are incredibly versatile. A little like a salad, you can use them as a topper for greens, stuff them in a pita shell or wrap, or eat them as is. This dish is best made in advance. It's easy to mix it up the night before or the morning of. The longer it sits, the more time the flavors have to develop. But you can, of course, mix it up and serve it immediately and it will still be great!

This is from my book *Sprouts for Your Food Storage* and is too good not to share again! Use this recipe as a base, adding any vegetables or meat you have on hand to dress it up.

- 3 tablespoons extra-virgin olive oil
- 2½ tablespoons red wine vinegar (or to taste)
- 1 tablespoon lemon juice
- 1½ teaspoons mustard
- 1½ teaspoons pure maple syrup, honey, or granulated sugar (or a drop or two of liquid stevia)

- 1 teaspoon sea salt (or to taste)
- ¼ teaspoon ground black pepper
- 1 to 1½ cups green onions (about 1 bunch), thinly sliced, dark and light green parts★
- ⅓ cup fresh parsley, minced★
- 1 cup tomatoes, diced (fresh or canned, well drained)
- 3 cups lentils, sprouted at least two days

In a large bowl, whisk together the oil, vinegar, lemon juice, mustard, sweetener, salt, and pepper. Stir in the green onions, parsley, tomatoes, and lentil sprouts. Season with additional salt and pepper to taste.

★Fresh green onions and parsley are fabulous, but you can also use dried versions. Dehydrated minced onions and/or chives (a couple of tablespoons) or dried parsley rehydrated and then drained well will work fine.

You'll find many more recipes for beans and legumes in my book *Stretchy Beans: Nutritious & Economical Meals the Easy Way*, plus how lentils and other beans work in our travel plans in *Real Food Hits the Road*. Although most of the recipes in those books don't fall under the no-cook umbrella, having a good number of bean recipes in your arsenal may be helpful.

Whole Grains

Wheat, rye, oats, rice, millet, barley, maize, and about 10,000 other species all fall under the category of cereal grains, are grasses. Supplies of grains have been a dominant theme throughout history and have kept the masses alive.

Wheat is mentioned numerous times in the Bible, often symbolically, serving as a metaphor for life, birth, and the resurrection. Pharaoh dreamed of "Seven heads of grain, healthy and good, were growing on a single stalk. After them, seven other heads of grain sprouted—thin and scorched by the east wind. The thin heads of grain swallowed up the seven healthy, full heads." Through God, Joseph interpreted Pharaoh's dream as seven years of abundance followed by seven years of famine.

The Roman Empire colonized many areas for their grain, which was the main sustenance for the city of Rome and its one million inhabitants. Grain, and later bread, was doled out at reduced prices or given for free. There's even some thought cereal crops, or more specifically the land needed to grow them, may have played a part in World War II, The Cold War, and the collapse of the Soviet Union.

Throughout history, grain has played an important role. The proper preparation of grains is important. Dr. Price noted in his studies that the introduction of white flour to what he referred to as "Primitive People" was a cause of tooth decay and deteriorating health. He did find many healthy societies who consumed grain—grains that were properly prepared.

Bread is likely the most common use of grains like wheat. Traditionally, the ground (or milled) grain would be traditionally leavened, now commonly called sourdough. Commercially available yeast is a relatively new invention. I'll admit, I'm a huge fan of sourdough bread and believe learning to make and work with your own sourdough starter is a valuable skill. I detail my love of sourdough in my book *Sourdough for Your Food Storage*. But for our purposes of no-cook meals, sourdough doesn't seem to be a good fit.

While it's true, sourdough should be cooked to be fully enjoyed, I've tasted my "raw" starter many times, and it's not bad! Add a little salt, and I may even go as far as saying it's good. Nutritionally, 1 cup of sourdough starter has approximately 432 calories, 2.1 grams of fat, 14 grams of protein, 91 grams of carbohydrates, and is a decent source of fiber and iron. Of course, this will vary depending on what you feed your starter. Some grains may have a higher or lower nutritional profile.

Eating your sourdough starter is a possibility, but please do check the section on Fuel-Saving and Low-Odor Cooking Methods for more options. Also, flour is considered a raw product that carries the risk of bacteria like salmonella or E. coli. The FDA recommends to not consume products containing raw flour, only cooked. They'd definitely frown on eating raw sourdough starter by the cup. Keep in mind, if low-odor guerrilla cooking is your goal, nothing smells quite like freshly baked bread. Especially to hungry people.

Like beans, whole grains can be sprouted. Also, like beans, grains contain phytase, which can bind with minerals in the body. Sprouting the grains helps reduce the phytase in the same manner we discussed earlier in this book.

I use the same colander method described in the Legumes section to sprout larger grains. For smaller grains, I use a fine mesh strainer instead of a colander. Wheat, rye, and barley sprout in about three or four days (depending on temperatures) and can be enjoyed raw. I absolutely love raw sprouted wheat! It's a tasty, slightly sweet, al dente snack. Different varieties of wheat do produce slightly different flavors. Sprouted hard red is my favorite, but soft white and hard white are also tasty.

Sprouted wheat can be steamed or lightly cooked and turned into a porridge, which would meet the preparation guidelines of the Weston A. Price Foundation. Even though I'm comfortable eating a portion of my sprouted wheat raw, WAPF believes all grains should be cooked for maximum nutrition, just like legumes.

Something to note about sprouting grains: they don't hold up well in the refrigerator. When you harvest and store them, at what you believe is the perfect tail and taste, you may find the tails have grown considerably in the cold—especially winter wheat varieties. It's ideal to sprout the amount you'll use within a short time, 24 to 36 hours, for the best flavor.

You can also let your sprouts grow out to become microgreens. If you find raw sprouted grains still too hard for your liking, consider microgreens. Growing your grains into grasses—you know the famous wheatgrass used in smoothies?—can give you a no-cook food.

Microgreens take about two weeks until they're ready to eat and can be used like sprouts or lettuce. If you have small or large livestock, you can set up large microgreen systems, sometimes called fodder systems. My chickens love wheatgrass! They also love heavily sprouted wheat (letting it go for up to a week).

Sprouting or growing grass is also a great way to *increase* your livestock grains. In fact, it's a great way to increase your human grains too. A cup of wheat will sprout to about 1½ cups, and ⅓ cup of wheat can be turned into about an 8" square of wheatgrass, which can be harvested up to three times.

When properly packaged, whole grains have a wonderfully long shelf life. Refer to the section Short-Term or Long-Term Storage for more information and recommendations. Keep in mind, while whole, intact grains have an almost indefinite shelf life, its lifespan is limited once you've milled it into flour.

Rice and millet can also be sprouted, as can quinoa. Once considered peasant food, quinoa has developed a reputation in recent years as a superfood due to being a high-protein plant food. Quinoa is a seed, commonly referred to as a grain or pseudo grain. For our purposes, I'm including quinoa in this section as opposed to the Seeds chapter.

These smaller grains need a fine mesh strainer for sprouting so they don't escape through the holes. Millet is usually purchased hulled, making it unpopular for sprouting. You could purchase millet sprays, popular among bird owners, if you are a sprouting purist.

I get unhulled millet. I soak and sprout it for a few days, tasting at each rinsing until it's the tenderness I'm looking for. While the sprouting performance is low, I've found many little tails and have been happy with the end result. My husband especially loves sprouted millet as part of a bowl of Muesli.

Sprouting rice is another grain with hit or miss results. Sometimes, my brown rice sprouts easily and lovely. Other times, not so much. Brown rice isn't common in food storage because of the germ, which can cause the rice to go rancid. I do keep brown rice, knowing its limited shelf life, and am diligent about the FIFO method. I'm comfortable keeping on hand what we'll use in 12 to 18 months. Brown rice can also be well-rinsed and used even if it is slightly past the best-by date.

White rice doesn't sprout since the germ has been removed, but I've fermented it and have drastically reduced cooking times. To ferment white rice, I soak it in clear water and add 1 tablespoon of sourdough starter (or another acidic medium, such as apple cider vinegar) per cup of rice. Soak for 12 hours, drain and rinse, then repeat the soaking and add fresh water and starter. Drain and then move to a mesh strainer and follow the sprouting process. Watch for the rice to bulge and develop a sweet yeasty smell, tasting at each rinsing.

Fermented rice will cook much quicker than its regular counterpart. White rice, with its long shelf life, is a very common food storage item, and it's certainly worth looking at multiple preparation methods for. Give the fermenting process a try.

Quinoa sprouts easily in a mesh strainer or mason jar with a sprouting lid. I've found older quinoa doesn't sprout as well as fresh quinoa, but it still develops small tails and is wonderfully soft and edible. When sprouting, be sure to taste your sprouts at each rinsing to get the taste you prefer.

The nutritional profile of soaked and sprouted quinoa is similar to cooked, coming in at 222 calories, 39 grams of carbs, 4 grams of fat, 8 grams of protein, and 5 grams of fiber per cup. Quinoa is also naturally gluten-free.

Officially, quinoa has a shelf life of approximately three years. But I'm currently using quinoa that was packaged in 2012 in mylar with oxygen absorbers. While slower to sprout, it is still fresh and tasty.

Quinoa is another one of my favorite travel foods since it sprouts easily and quickly. Check out *Real Food Hits the Road* for more info on how we eat away from home. Many of these tips and ideas can easily cross over to no-cook or low-cook food storage.

Oats are another popular whole grain food storage item. Oat groats are whole oats with the husk removed. This is the least processed version of oats. While oat groats can be sprouted, this isn't something I've tried since oat groats are not a large part of our food storage. Check the resources for a how-to link.

We do store other types of oats: rolled, quick-cooking, and steel cut. Each variety has its own merits. For your no-cook food storage, quick-cooking oats are a huge help. Rolled, also called old-fashioned, can also be utilized.

In recent years, overnight oat recipes have gained in popularity as a quick and healthy breakfast cereal replacement. Again, since oats are cereal grains, WAPF does not recommend eating them raw. That said, the overnight soaking does help reduce the phytic acid and makes them more digestible.

Personally, I find overnight oats, or Muesli, to be a delicious, fresh treat, especially during the summer months when I don't want a hot breakfast.

Fermented Oats

My friend Wardee has a fabulous 5-Minute Soaked Muesli Recipe (mix and match formula) on her Traditional Cooking School website (link in the Resources section). I love the ease of the formula and how it's so easy to take something simple and turn it into a new flavor experience with minimal effort.

These overnight oats are just as adaptable! Use these basic instructions and adjust to suit whatever you have on hand. Methods and formulas are a great way to save your food dollars by using items abundant to you, and it also cuts down on waste. My book *Design a Dish* expands on these formulas, giving the basics for making many meals and snacks by using your own ample ingredients and not having to run off to the store for a special element.

Soaking the oats, with the addition of an acidic medium, makes them more digestible than soaking in plain liquid and gives them the fermented quality. This results in a slightly tangy final product. If the tang is too much for you, skip the addition of the acidic medium. The overnight soak will still help with digestion and reducing the phytase in the oats.

Note: The acidic medium helps "protect" the oats during the fermentation process. I know some people are squeamish about leaving dairy products at room temperature (which is the standard when fermenting). I've never worried about this when using raw dairy since it sours instead of spoiling, but there is some validity to being concerned when using pasteurized/homogenized dairy (or reconstituted powdered dairy). If this is a concern to you, feel free to move it to the fridge for fermenting, knowing it may take longer and not be as digestible. You can also use water, Foundation Milk, or a nondairy milk for your liquid.

My oat preference for this, especially when fermenting, is rolled or old-fashioned oats. Steel cut oats don't break down enough, while quick oats break down a little too much.

That said, if you're looking for a thinner porridge as your end result, give the quick-cooking oats a try (not those little flavored packets, but plain ones). If you wish to use steel cut oats, increase the water by about one-quarter and be prepared to chew, chew, chew.

These oats have the addition of chia seeds or ground flaxseeds to help increase their creaminess. If you don't have or want to use these, decrease the liquid by about ⅓ cup.

This basic formula makes four ½-cup servings. When using whole milk, 1 tablespoon honey, and 2 tablespoons coconut oil, the nutritional profile is about 250 calories, 12 grams of fat, 6 grams of protein, and 24 grams of carbs.

- 2 cups milk of choice (fresh dairy, reconstituted dry, nondairy, plain water, or even my version of Foundation Milk described in the Dairy and Dairy Alternatives chapter)

- 1 tablespoon acidic medium (sourdough starter, apple cider vinegar, liquid whey, yogurt, or kefir)
- 1 cup rolled oats
- 1 teaspoon vanilla extract
- 2 tablespoons chia seeds or ground flaxseed
- A couple of pinches of sea salt
- 1 to 2 tablespoons of honey (more or less, or substitute maple syrup, or leave out and sweeten when ready to eat)
- 2 to 4 tablespoons coconut oil, palm oil, or mild olive oil or half that amount of MCT oil

In a medium glass bowl, mix the milk and acidic medium until well blended. Stir in the oats, vanilla, seeds, salt, and sweetener (do not add the oil at this time). Blend well and cover. Leave on the counter overnight and allow to ferment.

The next morning, taste and adjust as needed for sweetness. If your oil is liquid, stir in now. If using coconut oil not in its liquid state, warm it up a little and blend until smooth and creamy, then drizzle over the oats and stir in. Enjoy!

Tip: This base recipe can be scaled up or down. If you scale it up, you can keep it fermenting for several days, removing the amount needed each day. If you plan to keep it fermenting for several days, the only flavor add ins I recommend are dried fruit and/or nuts. Everything else should be added when ready to eat.

Flavor Ideas

The sky is the limit with additions for these oats. Dried fruit and/or nuts can be added before putting aside to soak. If using dried fruit, add a little extra liquid (a couple of tablespoons) to accommodate for the swelling of the fruit. Big pieces can be cut bite sized. Fresh or canned fruit can be added before or after soaking.

Even some vegetables work. How about shredded carrots, raisins, and a couple dollops of crushed pineapple for something like carrot cake? Or pineapple and shredded coconut with a little banana (fresh or chips) for a taste of the tropics?

Cocoa powder (plus a little extra sweetener) and/or peanut butter powder would work great when stirred in before eating. Or fresh peanut butter or chocolate chips (both?!). I love to add dehydrated blueberries or currents along with a dash of cinnamon and/or nutmeg when I start the soak. Delicious!

Prefer a Warm Breakfast?

These fermented oats can be made warm with the addition of boiling water. Since water has no odor when cooking, you'll have a near odor-free hot meal.

Here's how: decrease the liquid (milk or water) to 1½ cups. Proceed with the rest of the recipe as written (add in dried fruit or nuts to soak now). Allow to ferment overnight. Before adding the oil, stir in boiling water a cup at a time until it's heated through and is the consistency you wish. This ends up being a very creamy and smooth dish. Once the water is in, add any additional items you desire and stir in the oil. So good!

Noodles and Flakes

Pasta is one of the most popular dishes in the world. Noodles are inexpensive, versatile, and easy to prepare, plus they have a relatively long shelf life even with little change in packaging. Noodles, or pasta, are available in a variety of shapes and made out of an assortment of ingredients.

Because of sensitivity issues to wheat, for many years I ate gluten-free pasta made from rice instead of wheat. Now my gut has healed enough that the occasional bowl of regular wheat pasta doesn't bother me. That said, for those following a WAPF diet, brown rice pasta is preferred.

Noodles

While pasta may be inexpensive and easy, you may be wondering how it fits into your no-cook food storage. Afterall, those dried noodles—which may be edible—aren't tasty unless cooked. Surprisingly, certain varieties of noodles can fall into the no-cook category and almost all can be fuel-saving, low-cook foods. As a bonus, noodles are a low-odor food, making them suitable for guerrilla meals.

Angel hair pasta, also called capellini, which means "thin or very small hair" in Italian, cooks in boiling water in as little as two minutes. But did you know you can put it in room temperature water, let it soak for several hours, and end up with perfectly al dente noodles? It's true!

You will want to check the water a few times during the soaking to make sure the noodles are still covered, tasting at each check until they're the firmness you like. Al dente, the popular way to enjoy pasta, may be reached quicker than you expect. If you like your noodles soft, keep the process going until they are the way you want them.

Of course, it won't be hot pasta, but you can still enjoy a wonderful pasta salad. I especially like the angel hair pasta labeled as "perfect pot size" that's sold broken in half.

Another thin pasta we use for this soak-to-cook method is rice vermicelli, sometimes called stir-fry noodles. These thin noodles are found in the Asian section of the market and used for Thai dishes. With their great texture and mild flavor, these are my favorite for backpacking, camping, and hotel room meals. Like angel hair pasta, they take a few hours to soak (check the water during the process) before they're ready to turn into your favorite salad.

Other varieties of pasta can be used in a similar manner, but keep in mind, the thicker the pasta, the less likely it is to respond well to a long soak. I've found shapes like corkscrew soften much better when added to boiling water. Then you can turn off the heat and put the pasta in some sort of cozy (like a haybox) to keep warm, giving them time to soften in the hot water. The time needed will vary depending on the variety of pasta. Be sure to check out the Fuel-Saving and Low-Odor Cooking Methods chapter for more ideas on "cozy" cooking.

A few popular brands have started offering "quick-cooking" pasta. Available in a variety of shapes, they are advertised to cook in three minutes. They cook quicker because they are thinner than the conventional pasta in the same shapes. I haven't tried these, but if you're a fan of popular shapes like elbows, rotini, and penne, they may be worth searching out and experimenting with using the cold-soak method.

In addition to noodles, we store instant rice and couscous—again, in reasonable amounts that fit into our life. Both of these work well for the soak-to-cook method, with couscous taking as little as half an hour to rehydrate.

Instant ramen noodles are also suitable for soaking, but the nutrition of these little packs of noodles is lacking, especially when using the sodium and MSG-laden flavor packs. If using ramen for the convenience factor, consider searching out low-sodium varieties or tossing the flavor pack and seasoning with your own spices and sauces.

Confession time! My son, who has been raised on a traditional and real food diet, loves ramen. He prefers the type found in a ramen restaurant or the times I make it using better-quality rice noodles, but he also enjoys the little packages.

He's become quite the gourmet ramen chef, cooking his noodles in homemade bone broth, adding leftover vegetables and meat (or cooking an egg in the broth), and seasoning with spices and a dash or three of soy sauce. While still not up to WAPF standards (because of the steamed and then fried noodles), it's a lunch I'm fine with him enjoying on occasion. And I love he's taken such an interest in creating a dish he enjoys.

Although not a noodle or a flake, now's a perfect time to discuss rice paper or spring roll wrappers. Rice paper only needs to be submerged in warm water for seconds to become pliable. Fill with vegetables and/or meats, then roll up for something resembling a burrito or sandwich. Try these with my Peanut Sauce (recipe in the Nuts and Nut Butters chapter). Also check out Tuna Rolls in the Seeds chapter for filling ideas.

Another item worth mentioning is nori—the seaweed used in sushi. It's a great source of iodine, plus it works well for making not only a variety of regular rolls but also simple handrolls, which look a little like a cone. While canned tuna or salmon is great in these, you don't have to use any fish. Regular meats, eggs, or only vegetables work well. Even jerky can be used! Try a flavored mayo, like Sriracha Mayo, with these.

Since we're essentially talking about bread-free, no-cook "sandwiches," don't forget lettuce in place of a bun or bread. Low-carbers the world over have forgone the bread in favor of lettuce or cabbage leaves. The sky is the limit on fillings.

Flakes

This may get me banned from WAPF forever, but we also keep instant potato flakes on hand. In the same way my son enjoys ramen, I like instant potatoes. I don't know if it's a flashback to my childhood and school lunches or what, but they're a form of comfort food for me. While they are not a daily—or even weekly—part of our diet, I do make them enough to warrant adding them to our food storage.

This is a good time to remind you: store what you eat, eat what you store. While I may have an unnatural desire for instant mashed potatoes, if you don't like them it doesn't make sense for you to store them. Your food storage should be comprised of items you eat. This book is meant to offer ideas and allow you to think of no-cook (or low-cook) foods that make sense for you. Now back to the subject at hand . . . instant potatoes.

Not only do instant potatoes "cook" using the soaking method, but they do so quickly. Of course, the regular instructions are to simply boil water (with butter), add the flakes, and then turn it off to let it sit and thicken.

While hot mashed potatoes are my preference, we've had cold mashed potatoes on the trail, and I didn't hate them. Instant potatoes are popular with backpackers and ultrarunners since they're so quick and easy.

Backpackers often add additional items to make a full meal. There's even a dish referred to as Thanksgiving Dinner, which combines instant potatoes and instant stuffing with freeze-dried chicken and dried cranberries. While I'm not an instant stuffing fan (too much salt), this is another item that lends itself to no-cook or low-cook meals.

100

Ultrarunners just add water to the pouch, give it a slight massage to mix, then squeeze it into their mouths without missing a step. I can see the benefit of pouches of instant mashed potatoes in a sentry or patrol situation. They could be very convenient.

I suspect these noodle and flake ideas are just the tip of the iceberg when it comes to items that can be soaked to cook. You may already have thought of items you eat now that can utilize this method and become part of your no-cook food storage.

Nutritional Yeast

Not really a flake like potato flakes, but I wanted to mention this and couldn't find a spot, so here it is! Nutritional yeast is a highly processed deactivated yeast sold as a food product or supplement. Many vegans and vegetarians rely on nutritional yeast for protein, minerals, and B vitamins. It has a great cheesy, slightly nutty flavor and works nicely as a cheese substitute. In my house, we use it often in sauces, salad dressing, and as a popcorn topping.

While we have a nutritional yeast we like and use regularly, not everyone has the same experience. Most nutritional yeast is genetically modified and contains MSG. Before adding copious amounts of it to your food storage, explore whether this is right for you by researching brands and sampling them in small amounts. Start your research with the article "Why Nutritional Yeast is NOT Vegan Health Food {+ what it really is}" from Traditional Cooking School. You'll find a link in the Resources section.

Angel Hair Pasta and Marinated Tomato Salad

This is a delicious salad for your soaked angel hair pasta and comes together quickly with the addition of other food storage items. While written as a side dish to serve four to six people, you could easily turn it into a main dish for two with the addition of protein, such as canned chicken, salmon, or tuna. This is adapted from a recipe on The Pioneer Woman website, Angel Hair Pasta.

Marinated Tomatoes

- 1 can diced tomatoes, drained
- ¼ teaspoon garlic powder
- ½ teaspoon sea salt (you may need more if you use no-salt or low-salt tomatoes)
- ⅛ teaspoon red pepper flakes (optional)
- 2 tablespoons olive oil
- 2 teaspoons red or white wine vinegar

- 8 ounces angel hair pasta, cold soaked until al dente or to your desired firmness
- ¼ cup olive oil (a robust, highly flavored one is good in this)
- ¼ teaspoon garlic powder
- 2 teaspoons dried parsley
- 2 teaspoons dried basil
- Grated Parmesan cheese, whatever amount you desire—anywhere from a garnish to a light protein addition (optional)
- Sea salt, to taste
- Ground black pepper, to taste

Start with the marinated tomatoes to give them time to develop flavor. You could even mix this up at the same time you put the pasta in to soak.

Drain the tomatoes, reserving the liquid for another use. Sprinkle in garlic powder, sea salt, and red pepper flakes (if using). Mix to combine. Add the olive oil and vinegar. Mix again, then set aside until ready to use.

For the pasta, combine the dried parsley and basil in a small bowl. Add water to cover and let sit for a few minutes to rehydrate.

Drain the soaking water off the pasta, reserving the water. Shake your colander a few times to remove as much water as possible before transferring to a large bowl. *Pro tip:* always use a larger bowl than you think you need.

Add the olive oil, garlic powder, and rehydrated herbs to the pasta. Stir to combine. Add the Marinated Tomatoes and stir again.

Now you'll want to evaluate your pasta salad. Does it seem too dry? Add the reserved pasta water, a tablespoon or two at a time, to moisten. Once it's the consistency you desire, finish with optional Parmesan cheese and additional sea salt and pepper to taste.

If you still have leftover soaking water, it can be used in soups or sauces or to water plants.

Use this salad as a blueprint, changing the flavors by using different herbs and spices. I've made a salsa version of the Marinated Tomatoes many times by adding a little chili powder, cumin, and a dash of cayenne pepper and using lime juice instead of vinegar. You could swap Mexican oregano for the basil for a tasty south of the border style dish.

Rice Noodles with Peanut Sauce

This is another quick and easy trail food that lends itself to no-cook food storage. I use thin rice noodles for this. The thicker ones (used in pad Thai) will work but take longer to soften with the cold-soak method.

I've found breaking up the noodles before soaking makes for easier use in the end. I like to break them while they're still in the package (or vacuum seal) to cut down on the mess. Otherwise, they tend to go everywhere!

As written, this is a side dish and serves four to five people, or it can be a main dish for two. There's already some protein from the peanut butter powder, but it should be increased for a main dish. Add your favorite meat or consider adding collagen or whey protein if those are part of your no-cook food storage.

Read more about the nutrition of collagen and whey protein in the chapter Meal Replacement Powders and Supplements. If using collagen or whey protein, stir it into the sauce when adding the spices and herbs.

- 8 ounces thin rice noodles, cold soaked until al dente or to your desired firmness
- 2 tablespoons mild olive oil, avocado oil, or unflavored coconut oil in its liquid state
- ¼ teaspoon garlic powder
- 1 batch Peanut Dressing or Sauce (recipe in the Nuts and Nut Butters chapter)
- Sea salt, to taste
- Ground black pepper, to taste
- Optional toppings: red pepper flakes, Sriracha sauce, peanuts, sliced almonds, soy sauce, a dollop of sour cream

Drain the soaking water off the pasta, reserving the water. Shake your colander a few times to remove as much water as possible before transferring to a large bowl.

Add the olive oil and garlic powder to the rice noodles, then stir to combine and coat. Pour the Peanut Sauce on top, then gently lift and stir to combine.

Evaluate your pasta. Does it seem too dry? Add the reserved soaking water, a tablespoon or so at a time, until it's your desired consistency. Add salt and pepper to taste. If adding meat, stir it in now or let each person add their own.

Optional toppings can be added to the bowl or, my preference, each person can dress their own bowl or plate.

Variation:

We often make the peanut butter sauce and combine it with rice. This is one of my favorite dishes for using leftover rice, but it'd also work well with a batch of cold-soaked dehydrated or instant rice.

Flours and Meals

We keep a minimal amount of ground wheat flour on hand, preferring to store most of our grains whole. The shelf life of properly packaged whole grains, like hard red wheat kernels, is decades, whereas milled white flour is years. Don't get me wrong, years is still great!

If white flour is something you use regularly, you should keep some on hand for daily use and some stored for future use. Flour and similar powdered items store best when vacuum sealed and then stashed inside buckets.

How much you use on a weekly or monthly basis should be a guide for how much you store. Example, if you use 1 pound of white flour a week, storing 52 pounds will give you a year's supply. You could buy five 10-pound bags of flour (as I write this, the price listed at my local big box store is $3.64 a bag, for a total of $18.20 for 50 pounds) and a two-pound bag ($1.16), then repackage into 1-pound bags. With your one-year supply of flour on hand, use the FIFO method and buy a new pound each week. Yes, this is a rather simplistic way of having and rotating your flour, but it works.

Unfortunately, white flour doesn't provide much nutrition. There's a smidgeon of protein and iron but very little vitamins and minerals. There are some calories, about 110 per ¼ cup, but no fiber since the bran has been stripped away.

Whole wheat flour has a better nutrition profile and includes fiber since the bran remains, but it doesn't store as well as white flour. I like to keep a small amount of whole wheat flour on hand for ease of use, but again, the bulk of my "flour" is whole grains with a plan of milling as needed.

Reminder: If you store whole grains and plan to mill them, invest in a manual mill now. Small ones are less than $100 but do take some elbow grease to use. You'll spend several hundred on a decent manual mill. In the Whole Grains chapter, we discussed sprouting wheat and other grains. These sprouted grains can be dehydrated and then milled for sprouted flour.

Storing wheat flour definitely needed to be mentioned in this chapter, but this type of flour isn't really suitable for our no-cook needs. Eating this flour raw isn't very tasty—unless you use it to feed your sourdough starter, then the flavor is improved, but we can do better.

In addition to wheat flours not being tasty raw, there's the risk of bacteria like salmonella or E. coli. Wheat flour may not be suitable for no-cook use, but there are several alternative flours, with great nutritional profiles, that work well for our needs.

Almond Flour

Almond flour, also called almond meal, is almonds finely ground (or milled) into flour. You can do this yourself with a sturdy manual grinder and whole almonds (preferably ones that have been soaked and dehydrated—remember the phytase?). Or you can purchase almond flour already milled. Because of the natural fat in almonds, the flour doesn't have a "forever" shelf life.

With vacuum sealing and storing in a cool, dry, and dark location, I've kept almond flour fresh for over 18 months without issue. My guess is it'd be fine longer, but with my rotation system, I keep 18 months' worth on hand. Because of the natural oils, you'll know by the smell if almond flour is rancid. Spoiled almond flour may also taste off. If you're unsure, sample a small amount before using.

Because almond flour, even those that are labeled as raw, is made from pasteurized almonds (remember, all almonds sold in the United States are pasteurized by law; read more in the Nut and Nut Butters chapter) it's not a truly raw food like wheat flour and doesn't carry the risks of salmonella and E. coli in the same way, making it safe to eat without cooking.

Almond flour can be mixed up with a few simple ingredients to create no-cook energy bars (or balls), cookies, fat bombs, and more. Almond flour is high in nutrition, is gluten-free, and contains essential fats, protein, fiber, and assorted vitamins and minerals. It's a treasure trove of calories at 163 per ounce!

Coconut Flour

Like almond flour, coconut flour is safe to consume raw since the coconut meat used to make the flour is heated and dried before being ground. Also, like almond flour, the shelf life is limited.

Coconut flour is easy to digest and gluten-free. Two tablespoons have 60 calories, 2 grams of protein, 2 grams of fat, and 8 grams of carbohydrates—five of which are from fiber. Coconut flour's net carbs makes it popular among those following a primal or keto diet.

While this isn't a book about baking, I want to mention that baking with coconut flour is an adventure and takes some know-how. Most recipes require a lot of eggs to get a good consistency.

Bean Flour and Meal

As we've discussed, properly stored beans can remain fresh for years—decades even. But what if you're emptying out a cabinet and find a wayward package of beans tucked in the corner still in its original packaging?

You could soak and sprout a small amount as a test. If it sprouts, feel free to sprout the rest. If it doesn't sprout but only swells and bulges, you could probably get away with cooking the beans, but they may be tough. Adding a spoonful of baking soda during cooking may help soften the beans. Or you could grind the beans into a flour or meal for other uses.

Bean flour is gluten-free and fairly trendy. My Pinterest feed shows me new recipes for bean flours almost daily! The easiest use for bean flour is as a thickener in soups, stews, or gravies. It'll add the nutrition of the beans (remember that needed folate?) along with giving more substance to your dish.

You could use a mortar and pestle to grind beans into flour, but here's another instance where a decent-quality manual grinder will be a good investment.

Garden and Foraged Flours

Also filling my Pinterest feed are flours made from things like zucchini or foraged plants. Zucchini, or squash flour, is very easy to make and a great use for this often-prolific garden vegetable.

The squash is first shredded, then dehydrated until completely dry (either in a food dehydrator, a low-temp oven, or by using the sun), and then whirled in a food processor or high-speed blender until it's a powder. This is a great way to preserve extra garden squash now and add to your food storage.

Zucchini or squash flour can be mixed with other flours for baking or used as an addition to soups or stews for added vegetables. For our no-cook needs, they could be added to shaker smoothies.

Greens like spinach, kale, or leaf lettuce could also be dried and powdered into flour for use in soups, stews, or smoothies. Keep in mind the goitrogenic compounds, which increase the need for iodine in dark leafy greens like spinach and kale. Dehydrating these greens will not reduce this substance unless you first cook them at a simmer for 8 minutes, drain the excess liquid (squeeze it out), and then dehydrate.

There's a multitude of wild greens, grains, nuts, and more that can be foraged and processed into flours. Since we've already established foraging is not my forte, I'll refer you to the Resources section for articles where you can learn more.

Remember: Before handling any wild edible or medicinal, have the proper knowledge and resource consulting/learning from qualified sources.

No-Bake Chocolate Chip Cookie Dough

While no-bake, this is not entirely no-cook since it does use boiling water. This recipe makes about 18 tiny cookies and is an excellent source of healthy fat, at 6 grams per cookie, and approximately 90 calories in each. You even get about 2 grams of protein per cookie.

- ½ cup nut or seed butter (can use rehydrated peanut butter powder)
- 2 tablespoons coconut oil (in its liquid state) or 1 tablespoon MCT oil
- 2 tablespoons maple syrup (or 1 tablespoon honey)
- Pinch of sea salt
- 1 teaspoon vanilla extract
- ¼ cup boiling water
- ½ cup coconut flour
- ¼ cup mini chocolate chips

In a medium bowl, beat the nut butter until smooth. Stir in the coconut oil, maple syrup, sea salt, and vanilla. Add about half the water and stir until smooth. Add the remaining water and stir again.

When your batter is well blended, stir in the coconut flour. Let sit for 2 to 5 minutes so the coconut flour can absorb the liquid and thicken to a cookie dough like consistency.

Stir in chocolate chips.

Drop by teaspoons (or use a small cookie scoop) onto a plate. Eat right away or chill until firm.

Variations:

Leave out the chocolate chips for a plain cookie dough.

Omit the chocolate chips and add about a ½ teaspoon ground cinnamon for a Snickerdoodle type treat.

Increase the protein by adding collagen or whey protein powder to the dough. Stir it in before adding the water. You may need a little extra boiling water with these additions.

Almond Flour Pudding

This is another recipe that uses boiling or near boiling water. I often take the ingredients along with me when traveling for a quick breakfast or dessert. It's excellent topped with cream. If I don't have cream, I'll add extra hot water and maybe even a tad more coconut oil to make it a little smoother and creamier.

This is a single serving; scale up as needed. One serving has 400 calories, 37 grams of fat, and 10 grams of protein. You can increase the protein by adding collagen or whey protein powder before adding the hot water. You may need a little extra hot water with these additions.

- 2 tablespoons <u>hot</u> water
- 1 tablespoon coconut oil (or butter, ghee, or ½ tablespoon MCT oil)
- 1 teaspoon honey or 2 teaspoons dry sweetener or maple syrup
- 1 teaspoon molasses (optional)
- Dash of salt

- ½ cup almond meal

In a bowl, combine oil, sweetener, molasses, and salt. Pour hot water over the top and mix well with a fork or small whisk. When the coconut oil is melted or near melted, stir in the almond meal until smooth. When combined, allow to thicken for 1 to 2 minutes. Serve topped with fruit (if desired) and heavy cream.

Commercially Preserved

Dried fruit is a great ready-to-eat option. Combining dried fruit and nuts makes a handy trail mix. We keep a variety of commercially dried fruit on hand, including raisins, apricots, figs, dates, and coconut (both chips and shreds).

Depending on the fruit, the shelf life is anywhere from a year (again, when unopened and properly stored, this can just about double) to a decade or two. We've had unsweetened coconut shreds and chips vacuum sealed since 2012. I opened a package a few weeks ago, and it's still as fresh as the day it was purchased!

Nuts and dried fruits not only make a great trail mix but also a snack bar when whirled in a food processor. We have a solar system that gives us electricity even if the grid is down. (Unless there's an EMP. In that case, will the solar system survive the pulse? A question that doesn't seem to have a definite answer . . .)

But having a manual food processor is still a good idea. I've found soaking the nuts and seeds in water before processing makes the process go easier. It'll still take a little elbow grease but nothing like starting with unsoaked raw nuts.

Most dried fruit is high in concentrated sugars. When comparing fresh fruit to dried fruit by volume, there's more sugar and calories in the dried version, making them an ideal sweetener too. Fresh fruit may also be higher in some vitamins, but dried fruit is still a good source of fiber and minerals. Figs are high in calcium and are a great food option for helping reach your calcium needs.

Coconut flakes or shreds, as long as they aren't presweetened, are lower in sugar than other dried fruits while providing healthy fats and a good source of calories. Toasting coconut shreds in a dry skillet turns them into a wonderful treat. I also like to leave them untoasted, spritz them with a little water, then add seasoning for a wonderful snack. They are delicious sprinkled with curry powder.

When purchasing dried fruit, for the most natural choice look for unsulfured fruit dried at low temperatures (under 115°) without any oils or sugars added. Dehydrating at low temps retains more enzymes.

Commercially dried fruit is still very high in moisture and shouldn't be packaged in mylar with oxygen absorbers. Instead of leaving in its original packaging, vacuum seal dried fruit to extend its shelf life. If your original packaging had a best-by date, include that along with the date you vacuum sealed it on the label.

The key to long-lasting dried fruit is cool temps and lack of oxygen. Find a storage area with year-round temps lower than 60°. Create vacuum-sealed packages with the amounts of fruit that can be used within a few weeks once opened. Under proper conditions, your dried fruit shelf life can easily be 18 months to two years . . . officially. Unofficially, you might get the 10 plus years I'm experiencing with my dried coconut flakes and shreds.

Even though this section specifically focuses on commercially dried fruit, be sure to check the Home Preserved chapter for more information on drying your own fruit at home and how to store it.

Cans and Jars

Canned goods, a staple in most kitchens, are easily opened and enjoyed. Most are heated but almost all can be eaten without cooking. Any vegetable or fruit you can imagine is a likely addition to your no-cook food storage, as are canned beans—including baked beans—and canned meats and fish.

Most commercially canned goods have a shelf life of just about forever. Ensure the cans are not damaged or bulging, and it's likely the food inside is just fine.

What cans should you stock for your no-cook pantry? Just about anything you enjoy eating! Even with the long shelf life, it's still important to practice FIFO and to store what you eat and eat what you store. Otherwise, you may find yourself going through your shelves in five years and wondering what in the world you were thinking. Did you really plan on adding canned ox tongue to your next charcuterie board?

Canned foods are often touted as unhealthy and best to be avoided. The Weston A. Price Foundation lists canned fruits and vegetables on their Dietary Dangers list. While it's true fruits and vegetables are best in their most natural form, realistically, we can't always count on these.

Some of us (me!) may live where we can't grow fresh food year-round and the only option is the grocery store. I'll tell you, some months, the grocery store produce in my area is nothing short of sad. The shelves are empty, and what is there looks like it was on a truck for a week or two before reaching me—and it probably was.

Because of our location, we do reach for either frozen or canned produce as an alternative. We're not the only ones. Research shows people who rely on canned, as opposed to fresh, have a higher intake of fruits and vegetables plus higher nutrient intake (source 4). While I still believe fresh is best, I no longer shun canned goods in my pantry or as part of my no-cook food storage plan.

Because canned goods are often higher in salt, I gravitate toward low-sodium or no-salt varieties. For canned fruits, I look for no sugar added and avoid those in heavy syrup. Another thing I watch for is MSG. I once found these amazing looking canned greens that I thought would

119

be great for my food storage, until I read the label. Monosodium glutamate, commonly referred to as MSG, was right at the top.

Some nutrition is lost in the canning process. During the canning process, produce is peeled, which reduces the fiber content. Some vitamins, including vitamin C, are destroyed with the high heat of canning. On the flip side, other vitamins and nutrients not only survive the canning process but are enhanced. This is the case with lycopene, an antioxidant found in tomatoes that is better released when the vegetable is cooked (okay, yes—tomatoes are really a fruit).

In addition to fruits and vegetables, you can find many other food categories in cans or jars: beans, soups, dairy and dairy alternatives, condiments, and more. While I poked a little fun at the canned ox tail, canned meats are very popular. Chicken, ham, beef, processed meats, and especially fish are easy to find in any grocery store or online.

I'm particularly partial to canned fish—salmon, tuna, sardines, clams, and anchovies all have a prominent place in my no-cook food storage. Because of our local resources, we buy little other commercially canned meats. Your situation may be different, and you may choose to focus on a variety of canned meats in addition to canned fish.

Ounce per ounce, meat-based proteins tend to be higher in cost than plant-based proteins. Buying caseloads of canned beef will cost you more than buying bulk bags of pinto beans and white rice. For a more economical option, you may want to preserve meat at home. I give an overview of different home-preservation methods in the chapter Home Preserved. You can also use meats as a condiment to your plant-based proteins instead of the main ingredient.

When building your canned goods pantry, stick with the basics—the items you reach for in your daily cooking. This will help ensure your proper rotation (FIFO). Here's a partial list of canned and jarred fare to get you started.

Vegetables (look for low-salt or no-salt options to reduce the sodium content)

- Tomatoes
- Green beans (regular cut and/or French cut)
- Corn
- Carrots
- Peas
- Spinach
- Mushrooms
- Asparagus (regular and/or pickled)
- Artichokes (regular and/or pickled)
- Beans (pinto, garbanzo, refried, baked, etc.)
- Green chilis, jalapeños, pepperoncini, and similar
- Olives, pickles, etc.
- Beets (regular and/or pickled)

Fruits (avoid heavy syrup if sugar is a concern)

- Peaches (chunks, sliced, halves, etc.)
- Pears (chunks, sliced, halves, etc.)
- Pineapple (crushed, tidbits, chunks, slices, etc.)
- Pumpkin
- Cranberry sauce (gelled or whole)
- Fruit cocktail or other fruit mixes
- Mandarin oranges
- Apricots
- Grapefruit
- Cherries
- Apples
- Applesauce (also in convenient pouches and individual cups)

Meat and Fish

- Chicken
- Beef
- Tuna (I like a variety of styles, both in water and oil, plus pouches)
- Salmon (I like both the large cans and the smaller salad-style cans, plus pouches)
- Sardines (I like the ones in olive oil; my husband likes his in mustard sauce)
- Kipper snacks/herring filets
- Anchovies (salty goodness! I keep anchovy paste also)
- Smoked oysters
- Processed meats (usually very high in preservatives and sodium)

Miscellaneous (some of these may be listed or mentioned in other chapters)

- Coconut milk
- Soups (ready-to-eat and/or condensed)
- Jams, jellies, and preserves
- Pasta sauces
- Canned tamales (I hate to admit how much I like these things)
- Brown bread in a can (another guilty pleasure)
- Flavoring sauces such as soy sauce or hot sauce
- Hearts of palm pasta (low-carb pasta in a can)

Commercially Freeze Dried

While the bulk of our food storage consists of common everyday items, we do keep a small assortment of freeze-dried foods on hand. Most of these are in #10 cans and are individual items as opposed to meals, things like freeze-dried chicken, sausage crumbles, black bean burger, corn, mixed vegetables, strawberries (and other fruit), and the like.

Larger chain stores, and even a mom-and-pop store in my area, conveniently carry a small assortment of these long-term, prepackaged foods. This is a huge help and saves on shipping costs. That said, ounce per ounce, the cost of freeze dried is often much higher than canned, frozen, or fresh foods.

These freeze-dried items are convenient and truly are for long-term storage, with a super long shelf life of 20 to 30 years. Because of the long shelf life, these are one of the few things we do purchase and forget, instead of adding them to our regular FIFO rotation.

We do use individual freeze-dried meals, which are handy for backpacking, camping, and hunting trips. Because many of the meals are high salt and highly processed, we prefer not to rely on them for multiday events, but they work well for an overnight trip.

There's a wide variety of freeze-dried food available from a huge assortment of retailers. The quality also varies. There're a few very famous retailers who tend to have good quality across the board, and the cost of their items reflects this. You can find less expensive freeze-dried retailers but may sacrifice taste.

I found a "great deal" from a lesser-known company and purchased a small 72-hour kit (supposedly enough food and calories to last three days). We decided to take a few of the packages on a two-week camping adventure, figuring they'd make quick meals after a day of hiking.

After a long day, we made a family-sized broccoli cheddar soup in camp. While the meal did come together quickly, it was blah tasting at best, and I had to drink about a gallon of water in the middle of the night from all the salt.

My suggestion is to sample a small amount (such as a 24- or 72-hour prepackaged kit) before going all out and buying a pallet of freeze-dried food. Or do what we do and sprinkle in a freeze-dried meal, understanding they'll be a convenience and not the norm.

Be aware that freeze-dried meals tend to not only be high in sodium, but they also tend to be low in calories and protein. Many prepackaged, multiday kits allow only 1,500 (or less) calories per day. This may be enough if you're completely sedentary, but will it be enough if you are gardening, chopping wood, hunting, or walking patrol? What about pregnant or nursing mothers?

Adding additional ingredients to the freeze-dried meals may be necessary to balance out the nutrition. You could do this with your other food storage items or more freeze-dried ones in the form of individual items instead of meals. There's a wide assortment of freeze-dried meats and vegetables (usually available in #10 cans) and fruits (also in cans or sometimes mylar packages).

The freeze-dried broccoli cheddar soup we had while camping would've benefited from the addition of freeze-dried sausage crumbles and some spices. It wouldn't have helped the salt issue, but it would've been more satisfying.

While I wasn't a fan of that broccoli cheddar soup, I have found a few dry packaged soups—not labeled for long-term storage—that work well for camping and backpacking while doubling as short-term food storage. And, in my opinion, they're a much tastier option than some of the long-term storage soups.

These mixes often only need the addition of boiling water and a few minutes to absorb. You could even make the soup with cold water to make it truly no-cook, though you will sacrifice some flavor. They are advertised as family packs and usually offer eight servings, with each serving typically being under 200 calories. They also tend to be low in protein and fiber while high in carbohydrates.

The one package has been the basis of a meal for my family of three on several camping trips with the addition of sides. Again, it's not something that fits into our everyday eating plan, but it works well when needed.

In addition to freeze-dried, we keep several commercially dried or dehydrated items in our food storage. In previous chapters, we've already discussed dried milk and instant potatoes—two popular dehydrated food storage items. For some, dried beans are also considered to fall under this category.

Many foods with the "instant" label are items that were dehydrated and are reconstituted with water. Some examples are instant oatmeal or rice, instant noodles (ramen), instant breakfast, instant soup, instant coffee, etc. "Powdered" is another popular label, including powdered eggs, powdered creamer, and many more.

While the bulk of these are highly processed, many are worth considering for your no-cook food storage, even when leaning toward a whole foods diet. The convenience of the items is hard to beat.

Soaked Nut and Fruit Balls

In 2009, I was new to traditional foods. A friend of mine, who had a blog called GNOWFGLINS at the time, shared a homemade Larabar recipe. I'd never even heard of Larabars—a popular fruit and nut bar—but they looked so good! I quickly ran out, bought the ingredients, and tried it. Delicious!

Over the years, I've tweaked the original recipe to better suit our needs and use a manual food processor. (The recipe is still available on the blog, which is now titled Traditional Cooking School, and the blog owner, Wardee, has become a dear friend over the years.) Be sure to check below the recipe for add in and flavor ideas.

- ½ cup dates
- ½ cup dried fruit (such as raisins, craisins, figs, apricots)
- ¾ cup nuts (preferably raw; almonds are my go-to for this, but feel free to try other nuts or combinations of nuts)
- Water (for soaking)

- 2+ teaspoons sea salt, divided
- 1 tablespoon cocoa powder or peanut butter powder (optional)
- ¼ cup add ins (shredded or flaked coconut, chocolate chips, sunflower seeds, pumpkin seeds, lemon zest; optional)
- Additional water or lemon or lime juice (optional)
- Toppings to cover the finished treat (sesame seeds, finely shredded coconut, cocoa powder, finely chopped nuts, oats, etc.; optional)

In a medium to large bowl, combine dates, dried fruit, and nuts. Smooth out so they're flat but allow them to remain loose (don't pack down the fruit and nuts). Add enough water to cover the nuts and fruit plus about ½ inch over the top. Add 1 teaspoon of sea salt. Stir to incorporate. Cover with a dish towel and set on the counter for 8 to 12 hours.

At the end of the soaking time, drain off the water with a colander. Give the nuts and fruit a couple of good shakes to remove excess water.

Move to a food processor. Add the remaining teaspoon of sea salt. Process until a paste is formed. If using a manual processor, this may take a few minutes. Do this in batches if your processor isn't large enough for the quantities listed.

Transfer from the processor to a bowl.

If you're using nuts, large seeds, or coconut flakes as your add ins, give them a quick whirl in the processor if you'd prefer them broken up.

Now you have the option of returning everything to the processor and pulsing while adding in the rest of your add ins, or leaving it all in the bowl and using a wooden spoon and a strong arm as you flavor your nut and fruit balls. If the mixture is too dry to hold together, add a little liquid, a teaspoon or two at a time. This liquid can also be part of your flavoring.

If you're using topping(s), get this ready now. Put your finely shredded coconut, sesame seeds, cocoa powder, very finely crushed nuts, or other toppings on a plate. If using multiple toppings, separate each on its own plate.

Go back to your fruit and nut combination. If everything is well mixed and combined, form into walnut-sized balls. Next, roll each ball in your topping to fully cover, or only partially cover if you prefer. Some toppings, like coconut, seeds, or nuts, can be lightly pressed in.

Place on a plate or in a pan and cover to keep them from drying out. These will keep for a day or two at room temp, longer in the fridge.

Variation: Press into a pan, cover with wrap and cool for several hours before cutting into bars.

Flavor Combination Ideas:

- Lemon: add a few teaspoons of fresh lemon zest or 1 teaspoon dried lemon peel powder. Use lemon juice for your additional liquid.
- Choco/Coconut: use cocoa powder, coconut (either shredded or flakes whirled in the blender) and a few extra pinches of sea salt.
- Double Choco/Coconut: use cocoa powder, coconut (either shredded or flakes whirled in the blender), mini chocolate chips, and a few extra pinches of sea salt.
- Peanut Butter: use peanuts as your nuts (soak with the fruit) and add 1 tablespoon of peanut butter powder as an add in.
- Key Lime: add a few teaspoons of fresh lime zest or 1 teaspoon dried lime peel powder. Use lime juice for your additional liquid.
- Brownie: add cocoa powder and a tablespoon or two of mini chocolate chips. Chop up a few tablespoons of nuts into small pieces (walnuts or pecans are fabulous) and fold in.
- Cashew Perfect: use cashews as your nut. Add an extra pinch of sea salt. That is all—perfect and delicious!

- Peanut Butter Chocolate Chip: use peanuts as your nuts (soak with the fruit). Add in 1 tablespoon of peanut butter powder and a few tablespoons of mini chocolate chips.

Variation: Unsoaked Nut and Fruit Balls

This works great with an electric food processor. My tiny manual grinder/processor does not have enough oomph for starting with unsoaked nuts and fruit.

Use the ingredients and amounts listed for the soaked version of Nut and Fruit Balls, just skip the soaking step.

Put the dried fruit, dates, and nuts in the food processor. Add 2 teaspoons of sea salt. Process until a thick paste is formed. Proceed with add ins and flavorings as desired. You may need extra liquid to get the balls/bars to hold together properly.

Sardine Salad

I tiptoed into sardines by treating them like tuna and making a salad. I already knew about the benefits of sardines: an excellent source of Omega-3 fatty acids, selenium, calcium, and phosphorus, along with being high in protein and a natural source of vitamin D. They are also low in mercury, inexpensive, and sustainably caught.

I chose sardines canned in olive oil for my first salad. They were amazingly mild—not at all what I expected. They were so mild, my husband didn't even realize we were eating sardines and not tuna. Now we often eat sardines on their own, on crackers, or atop a green salad. I still prefer sardines in olive oil, but my husband likes them in mustard sauce.

We've tried a variety of different brands, and like everything, some are better than others. The large sardines (in a large can) in tomato sauce were a solid no from all of us. We stick with the small tins.

I read an article years ago about how a single sardine can work with the other foods in your diet and provide extra nutrients. I've lost the article and wasn't able to find a copy on the World Wide Web, but other resources convince me of the health benefits of sardines. Try them! You may love them too.

This is adapted from Edible Aria and serves two. Each serving (sardine salad only) is around 200 calories, with 15 grams of protein and 12 grams of fat.

- 1 tin of wild-caught sardines in olive oil, partially drained (olive oil can be reserved for another suitable use)
- 2 tablespoons mayonnaise (homemade preferred)
- 1 tablespoon dried chives
- 1 tablespoon capers, no juice (or substitute dill relish)
- 1½ tablespoons lemon juice
- 1 to 2 pinches dried dill
- 2 teaspoons dried parsley
- 1 teaspoon mustard or ¼ teaspoon mustard powder
- Sea salt, to taste
- Ground black pepper, to taste

Add the sardines and oil to a medium glass bowl. Add remaining ingredients except salt and pepper. Toss gently to break up the sardines. Season with salt and pepper to taste.

Allow to set for several minutes for the flavors to blend and meld. Serve as a sandwich, as a filling in nori or rice paper, or as the protein in a lettuce, grain, or bean salad.

Home Preserved

Home preservation is a great way to ensure the food you have on hand is exactly what you want to eat. By home canning, dehydrating, freeze drying, curing, and even freezing, you can fill your larder with little to no compromise.

For most home-preservation methods, there is some upfront investment. This may be under $100 or up to several thousand. There's also a need for the knowledge to preserve properly and safely.

As the scope of this book is no-cook food storage, I'm sharing the basics as it relates to this subject. You'll want to pursue additional information to become proficient in these methods. There're tons of resources available!

My family harvests the bulk of our meat at home, along with a smattering of produce. We also get produce from either local farmers or friends and/or buy in bulk when given the opportunity. Farmers' markets or direct from the farm are often excellent resources for stocking up. Asking for seconds or gleaning already harvested fields and orchards can result in great deals.

Because everything tends to be ready at once—gardens are ready to pick at the same time hunting season begins—we look for simple methods to preserve the harvest. These home-preserved items are a large component of our food storage plan. Many of these preserved foods also work well for no-cook food storage.

Here are a few preservation methods we've used on our small homestead:

- Freezing
- Canning—both pressure and water bath
- Dehydrating

- Fermenting
- Salt curing (meats and herbs)
- Alcohol immersion
- Olive oil immersion (limited because of safety concerns and the need for refrigeration)
- Cold storage (root cellar, pseudo root cellar)

And while we don't do this, you can also freeze dry at home. I loved the idea of having complete control over the ingredients and potentially saving money in the long run, but the cost of a home freeze dryer has us currently sitting out on this method.

I did run the numbers, thinking we could find some savings by not purchasing commercially freeze-dried items, but with the minimum amount of freeze-dried food we store, we aren't convinced a freeze dryer is right for us. That said, I know several people who've purchased and love them, feeling they are well worth the money.

One of my favorite websites with information on freeze drying is Common Sense Home. If you think a home freeze dryer may be right for you, I'd recommend reading their article "Home Freeze Drying – Read this Before You Buy a Freeze Dryer" (link in my Resources section). This article shares all the information you need when considering this major purchase.

Freezing

Our go-to storage method for the bulk of our harvest is freezing. We have two chest freezers, along with the bottom freezer in our refrigerator. My husband is an expert stacker and really makes the most of our available space.

Many people discount using their freezer for food storage. I'm not one of those people. I truly believe a freezer is excellent for food storage as long as you have a plan for *if* the freezer is not usable. You may remember in the Introduction chapter my friend whose family lived on food storage for a year while out of work. The freezer was working just fine during that time.

One of our chest freezers is located by an outlet that connects to our solar system. The other is in the garage on grid power. For a power outage similar to the one we experienced during the 2007 gale, we have a generator (and fuel) to keep the garage freezer frozen.

If we experience a major event with a long-term power outage that surpasses our stored fuel and/or an event that took out our solar system, we'd be turning to canning, nonelectric dehydrating, fermenting, salt curing, and possibly alcohol and olive oil immersion.

Remember, a full freezer stays cold and uses less energy than an empty freezer. As you eat the freezer foods, consider putting buckets or jugs of water in the available space. While a fuller freezer is helpful, you also don't want it *too* full. There should be room for the air to circulate.

Canning

I'd never canned before our preparedness and traditional food journey began. I knew it was a skill I wanted to add to my arsenal and was blessed to have a friend teach me. I also purchased *The All New Ball Book Of Canning And Preserving* to use as a reference guide. Under her tutelage and armed with my book, I was a canning maniac. I started with water bath canning before moving on to pressure canning.

Learning what is safe to water bath can and what must be pressure canned is important. *The All New Ball Book Of Canning And Preserving* will give you the details you need to safely can and prevent foodborne illnesses such as the potentially fatal botulism.

Learning how to pressure can has been a wonderful thing. It's great to have additional options for preserving the meat we harvest yearly. I love to raw pack chunks of deer or antelope. The end result is the most tender and amazing meat ever. It's great to add to soups, stews, stroganoff, and more.

When I first began pressure canning, the recommendation was to boil the canned meat for 10 minutes before using. This meant you weren't supposed to eat it straight from the jar. That recommendation has changed, and provided proper techniques are followed, it is now deemed safe straight from the jar. This makes your home pressure canned meat safe to add to your no-cook food storage plans. Woot-woot!

Dehydrating

Dehydrating is another skill I worked on during that time. I was slightly more familiar with dehydrating than canning, thanks to my Great-Aunt Retha. She dehydrated each summer using a simple screen setup. This was much like a pair of screen doors with a base to make them counter height.

She'd lay out thinly sliced fruit from her orchard on the bottom screen and cover it with the top screen, allowing them to dry in the sun for several days. She'd monitor the fruit and flip it as necessary. I was completely fascinated with the process! I tend to rely on an electric dehydrator for ease of use, but I have the materials to build my own screen-based dehydrator if needed.

My electric dehydrator is nothing special. I spent less than $50 on it a dozen years ago. It's still working great and is exactly what I need. I've dehydrated bushels of fruits and vegetables, along with pounds upon pounds of jerky. When my two youngest daughters (now adults) were still at home, I made jerky almost weekly for them to take in school lunches.

Home-dehydrated foods, especially fruits and vegetables, need to be conditioned before moving to storage. When dehydrating, not all pieces dehydrate at the same rate. Thinner pieces may be dryer than thicker pieces, or the trays may not have been rotated properly and dried unevenly. It's even possible some of the fruit started with more moisture in it. You need to condition the food to make sure the humidity level is equal throughout to prevent spoilage.

The first step toward conditioning is making sure your food—fruits, vegetables, meat, nuts, herbs—is properly dried. If using a recipe, follow the instructions for timing and testing. In the Resources section, you'll find links to two separate articles: "How do I Know When Fruit is Dry?" and "How do I Know When Vegetables are Dry?"

To condition, move the cooled, dehydrated food to jars—not necessarily the jars you plan to store in. You want to pack the dried food in loosely, leaving some space at the top. Then put on the lid. Place the jar(s) in a visible location, and each day, shake and move the jar, allowing the food to move around freely.

Check the jar for any signs of moisture, food sticking together, or food sticking to the jar. If things are sticking, give it a shake and, if it comes loose, it's probably fine. Check again the next day. If it doesn't easily come loose, return to the dehydrator. Check your jar daily for 7 to 10 days.

During these 7 to 10 days, if you see any signs of mold, discard the entire contents of the jar. Mold is often caused by not properly drying. At the end of the conditioning time, you can then properly package your dehydrated food for shelf storage.

Home-dehydrated fruit is dryer than the commercial varieties, but they still store best when vacuum sealed, as do dehydrated vegetables. Another bonus of home-dehydrating produce is being able to powder the dried items.

Fruit powders are excellent to add to hot cereal, yogurt, smoothies, and more. Dehydrated and powdered zucchini makes a great flour, and tomato powder is wonderful to make into paste and sauces. Powdered greens can be added to smoothies, soups, broth, and sauces. And since you're preserving at home, you can simmer the greens, drain well, and then dry them to reduce the goitrogenic compounds for increased benefits.

In addition to dehydrating sliced fruit and vegetables, we also dehydrate beans (usually mashed then dehydrated), grains, fruit leather, and various barks.

Soaking and cooking your own beans, then mashing and dehydrating them, makes a great quick-to-use bean dish. Just add water and cold soak to rehydrate.

Cooked then dehydrated rice makes a quick side. It also rehydrates with a cold soak in only a few hours. You could make this for a slightly healthier version of instant rice. Brown rice can be cooked and dehydrated, too, but it should be kept in the freezer and used within a short while. Jasmine and basmati are both very tasty when dehydrated.

I mentioned yogurt bark in the chapter on Dairy and Dairy Alternatives. Yogurt dries wonderfully. One cup of yogurt ends up being only about ½ cup when dried. It can be reconstituted with water or eaten as is. You can also get creative with the yogurt and include puréed fruit during the drying process.

Other useful "barks" include potato, sweet potato, tomato, pumpkin, and many more. These can be used like the yogurt bark and reconstituted or even be eaten dry—they're a little like a chip. Salsa or Sriracha bark is excellent for adding extra flavor to just about anything. For more bark ideas and how-tos, plus information on dehydrating full meals, visit Backpacking Chef online.

Dehydrating jerky at home also provides excellent options. You can marinate it in your preferred sauce with your preferred ingredients, knowing exactly what you are getting. Your jerky can be made from strips or from ground meat, using any meat you choose.

Because we harvest wild game, our jerky is usually made from deer or antelope (pronghorn) and occasionally elk or beef. I've considered making chicken jerky but have yet to do so. I've also turned my jerky into pemican by powdering the well-dehydrated meat and then mixing with dried fruit and fat.

We recently added a smoker and are beginning to experiment with using it to make jerky. A neighbor makes the best goose jerky in his smoker. I'm not a huge fan of goose, but it's pretty amazing when made into jerky.

Home-dehydrated jerky is not recommended for pantry storage. It can be kept in the refrigerator for about a week or stored in the freezer for six months. Even with needing to store jerky in the freezer, I still find it to be a useful method to save space. Dehydrating meat reduces its size to about a quarter of the original volume.

In addition to jerky, we've also tested dehydrating ground meat, often called "gravel" in dehydrating circles. Lean ground beef (or wild game, in our case) is mixed with breadcrumbs, browned, rinsed, blotted to remove excess fat, then dehydrated. The breadcrumbs make the meat less gravel-like.

It was fine, but we didn't enjoy the "gravel" enough to make it a regular part of our food preservation repertoire. For the work involved, I'd prefer to pressure can the meat. It's much more usable.

Fermenting

Fermenting is another excellent preservation method, especially for vegetables. I suspect we're all familiar with sauerkraut—which translates to "sour cabbage" in German. Sauerkraut is simply finely shredded cabbage that has been lacto-fermented. When properly made and stored, it has a shelf life of a year (maybe longer) and seems to get even better with age. I've heard stories of German families who had large crocks of kraut in the basement, put up every year at harvest, and preserved to enjoy until next year's harvest.

My fermenting is on a smaller scale, using simple (inexpensive) mason jars. But they're still wonderful and long lasting. Learning to ferment opens up a whole new world of preservation.

While it's ideal for cabbage, it also works well for carrots, greens, turnips, beets, and much more. And within the individual vegetables, you can create many flavors. Cabbage can be made into traditional German-style sauerkraut with simple seasonings, or with a few slight changes, the same cabbage can be converted to a spicy Kimchi. Carrots can be fermented as coins with garlic or shredded with ginger. There are so many options!

Lacto-fermentation is not only an excellent preservation method, but it's also a great way to add live and active probiotics to your diet. These are imperative for good gut health and can promote wellness—important things in time of stress. Most fermented foods are eaten straight from the jar, making them a perfect choice for your no-cook food storage.

Fruits can also be fermented, but they don't have the shelf life vegetables do. Because of the natural sugars in fruit, if left to store too long, you'll end up with wine. Even so, you can easily extend the fruits' life by several weeks and provide gut-friendly probiotics.

Tomatoes have a short shelf life. The acid in them makes them a little too tangy after a few weeks. Even so, fermented salsa is one of the best things ever. You must try it!

Besides fruits and vegetables, you can also ferment legumes, eggs, meat, fish, and a whole host of other items. Making cheese is even a form of fermenting. Just like home canning, there are specific practices to follow for safe fermenting: having the proper brine, clean containers and utensils, and quality produce or other foods, along with making sure the food is submerged and under the brine.

I highly recommend Traditional Cooking School's Lacto-Fermentation eCourse or eBook, where you can learn all about the wonderful world of fermenting.

An important component to fermentation is having a cool place to store the ferments. The refrigerator is the natural choice, but other options include a basement, root cellar, or a cold closet. When we lived in Central Wyoming, our north-facing bedroom closet was the perfect choice. It stayed cool year-round but not so cold it froze in the winter.

Salt Curing

One of the biggest concerns with food spoiling is bacteria. To grow, bacteria needs moisture. Thousands of years ago, some very smart people discovered salt prevents bacteria from growing by pulling out the moisture.

Homegrown herbs are a wonderful thing to preserve in salt. When done properly, by layering the salt and herbs in a jar, the herbs will remain fresh for months. Simply rinse or brush off the salt before use. You'll also want to use less salt in the recipe, due to salt remaining in the herbs.

Before refrigeration and canning, salt curing was the main preservation method for meat. There're many meats you may be familiar with today that have been traditionally salt cured to get their pronounced flavors. Salami, prosciutto, pancetta, pepperoni, and many more were salt cured. In today's world, the pepperoni or salami you buy in the local supermarket may not be made in the same manner, but their origins are based in salt curing.

So far, my experience of salt curing meat is limited to gravlax or salt-cured salmon. I've used the same method for salt curing trout, too, which worked very well. I've recently taken a course on dry-curing meat, which uses salt, and I hope to put it into practice with this year's wild game.

Alcohol Immersion

Alcohol can be used for preservation. Like salt, alcohol pulls out water and prevents bacteria growth, while also actively killing bacteria, yeast, and fungus. In order to get the full benefits, it's important to have the correct amount of alcohol for the quantity of food.

Vanilla extract is an example of alcohol preservation. You can use this same concept for making extracts out of a variety of herbs and fruits. Medicinal herbs are also added to alcohol to make tinctures. If you don't wish to use alcohol, you can make tinctures and extracts using glycerin. Check my Resources for more information on extracts and tinctures.

Vodka is commonly used for medicinal tinctures since it doesn't impart any flavor. If you want flavor, you could use brandy, cognac, or rum— depending on the desired end result. If you add an orange to brandy, you'll end up with a slightly different flavor than an orange added to cognac.

Preserving in alcohol isn't limited to extracts. You can preserve whole fruits or slices. Usually, when preserving the actual fruit, you'll have the addition of sugar. Like salt, sugar has a history of use in preservation, and it also works to draw out moisture.

Olive Oil Immersion

In the chapter on Dairy and Dairy Alternatives, I briefly mentioned making balls out of yogurt and storing them in olive oil. Olive oil has been used as a preservative since ancient times. The oil prevents oxygen from reaching the foods, which prevents bacteria . . . but not all bacteria. Botulinum toxin, commonly called botulism, lives in an anerobic environment, so oil preserving will not prevent it.

Because of botulism, preservation in oil isn't widely used, and it's not recommended. The USDA has a short article on the subject: "*Garlic, vegetable or herb in oil mixtures may support the growth of Clostridium botulinum bacteria. For safety reasons, they should be made fresh. Leftovers should be refrigerated for use within three days, frozen, or discarded.*" (source 6).

And a second article specifically asks, "*Can you get botulism from garlic in oil?*" Short answer: yes. Garlic in olive oil should be stored in the refrigerator for a maximum of seven days or frozen for several months. Storing at room temperature is not recommended.

For safety reasons, I only have a few recipes I preserve in oil and keep in cold storage, like my yogurt balls. These items work perfectly for our no-cook options, but because they are limited in their shelf life, they're not a good long-term storage food.

Cold Storage

When we were planning the build of a new house, we discussed starting with the root cellar. I'd found some interesting readings about pioneers in the plains who would build the root cellar first, giving them a cool place to escape the scorching sun and a warmish place to survive the winter. I wish we would've followed through with that discussion! After over six years of living in our new home, we still don't have a root cellar.

But I do have an unheated room attached to my house that works fairly well for keeping food during the winter. It stays just warm enough that it doesn't freeze—most of the time.

If we know we're going to have a severe cold snap, such as -20° or colder, we'll move some of the things we have stored to our guest room. This room is the farthest from the woodstove (we heat the entire house with wood, no central heating), and the door is kept closed during the winter. It works well as a backup. We keep things like potatoes, pumpkins, winter squash, carrots, turnips, and beets in our coldish rooms, storing enough of these items to take us through the better part of winter.

If you have a basement, this may work well as a root cellar replacement. You can also make a potato or root clamp, which is essentially a hole dug in the ground, lined with straw, then the vegetables are added along with more straw and a layer of dirt.

I've also heard of burying old freezers or tall metal garbage cans to use as pseudo root cellars. In some climates, you may be able to leave your root vegetables in the ground, cover them well with straw, and dig them as you need them. Cold frames may be another option for extending the amount of time root veggies can stay in the ground.

While cold storage is a useful food preservation technique, for our no-cook food storage, it's not overly necessary. Most of the items we store in our cold room need to be cooked. Carrots are the exception since they are delicious raw. And beets and turnips can be fermented and then eaten raw. Like most vegetables, you'll get plenty of nutrients from these items, but they are low on the calorie side.

Rice and Salmon Salad

This is a huge adaptation of a delicious recipe from Traditional Cooking School. I've been making this for over a dozen years, in some variation. This is also one of our favorite road trip meals.

I share a slightly different adaptation of this same recipe in my book *Real Food Hits the Road*. It works well with precooked and frozen rice, or rice cooked in a hotel room using a rice cooker, crockpot, or Instant Pot (we often take one of these options on road trips).

For the purpose of this book, we're using cold-soaked dehydrated rice. You can dehydrate soaked and cooked brown rice, which has a better nutritional profile, at home for your short-term food storage. Soaking brown rice, to reduce the phytic acid, and then cooking and dehydrating, gives you instant rice with more nutrients than the stuff you can buy in a box.

Because brown rice still has the bran, it doesn't keep as long as white rice. How long will your home-dehydrated brown rice last? When packaged without air (in mylar with an oxygen absorber or vacuum sealed), it should last for several months. For longer term, you can store it in the freezer. (Remember, dehydrating shrinks the product, so it will take up less space.)

Commercially packaged freeze-dried brown rice would also be a good choice for this recipe. Or use commercially purchased instant white rice. Because instant white rice is lacking in both nutrition and taste, focus on your add ins. I use the smaller (7.5-ounce) can of salmon in this recipe, but you can also use half or all of a 14.75-ounce can, or three packages of salmon in pouches.

This recipe is very basic, with lots of options to add or vary ingredients to what you have on hand and make it your own. Be sure to check out the original recipe from Traditional Cooking School in the Resources section.

- 1 cup plain yogurt, or rehydrated yogurt bark to equal 1 cup
- 2 tablespoons mayonnaise or mild olive oil
- ½ can diced tomatoes, drained
- 1 cup peas (fresh is best, thawed frozen is good, canned works, too; you could even use sprouted peas)
- 2 tablespoons dried parsley
- 1 teaspoon dried dill
- 1 teaspoon curry powder (more if you like curry)
- 3 tablespoons lime juice
- 3 cups prepared dehydrated or freeze-dried rice, cold soaked
- 1 (7.5-ounce) can salmon
- A few dashes of liquid smoke (optional)
- Sea salt, to taste
- Ground black pepper, to taste
- Additional add ins as desired or available (see ideas below)

In a medium bowl, combine yogurt, mayonnaise, tomatoes, peas, parsley, dill, curry powder, and lime juice. Mix to combine. Set aside for at least 10 minutes to allow the flavors to meld and the herbs to reconstitute. Give it a taste and add salt and pepper as desired.

Flake salmon into a separate bowl, removing (or crushing) bones as needed/desired. Add a few dashes of liquid smoke to give a smoked flavor to your salmon.

Put the prepared rice in a large salad bowl. Add the yogurt sauce and stir to combine. If you're using any additional add ins, stir them in now. If it seems a little dry, you can add additional yogurt, mayo, olive oil, or a little water or milk.

Give it a taste. Does it need more salt and pepper? A sprinkle of dill? Adjust the flavors to make it your own. Gently stir in the flaked salmon and enjoy.

Add Ins:

This recipe is fabulous for adding leftovers and bits of things.

- Any fresh salad-type vegetables, such as cucumber, green pepper, green onion, celery; cut into bite-size pieces
- Corn kernels
- Shredded carrot
- Avocado
- Sliced black olives
- Pimento
- Dill or sweet pickle chunks
- Capers
- Hard-boiled eggs, diced or sliced
- Sliced nuts, such as almonds
- Dried fruit such as raisins, craisins, or other fruit, cut into bite-size pieces

- Sprouted lentils or mung beans (as an addition to, or in place of the peas)
- Up the protein by adding collagen to the yogurt and mayo
- Chia seeds or ground flaxseed would also work as an addition to the dressing; you may need to increase the liquid slightly so it doesn't get too thick
- Poppy seeds would increase the calcium

Substitutions or Variations:

- You could substitute leftover chicken, beef, or pork for the salmon or use tuna instead.
- Instead of rice, you can use any grain as a base. Sprouted quinoa would be lovely and substantially increase nutrition.
- Instead of a dairy-based dressing, how about a mustard vinaigrette? This should pair nicely with the salmon.
- Change up the herbs as desired. Don't care for curry? Leave it out.
- Combine salsa and yogurt (or sour cream) for the dressing. Add a little chili powder, cumin, and as much cayenne as you dare for taco-flavored rice. You could stick with the salmon or switch to chicken or beef.
- Instead of using fresh yogurt or yogurt bark, substitute sour cream or reconstituted sour cream powder.
- This rice salad also makes a great taco filling. You could even try it in nori sheets, rice paper, or lettuce leaves.

Meal Replacement Powders and Supplements

In the past few years, we've added a variety of whey protein powder, collagen, gelatin, and a few other supplements to our food storage.

Whey Protein Powder

Whey protein powder is an easy, just-add-water food storage option. It's also great when added to oatmeal, rice, smoothies, mixed into protein balls, fruit and nut balls, and so much more.

But . . . whey protein powder is not WAPF approved. The protein in whey is fragile and can be damaged in processing. Plus, many are made from questionable ingredients. I look for a high-quality powder with minimal processing and no added sugar.

The cost of protein powder, even those with questionable ingredients, is on the high side. Expect the cost per serving to be $1 to $2 for the powder alone. You'll also want to sample a few different varieties to find one that has the flavor you like.

We have two we buy, one because the processing is top notch and from grass-fed cows; the other with slightly less preferred processing but still non-GMO from grass-fed cows and has better flavor. The second one is so good (to me) I often have it with just plain water. It's almost like a milkshake. And I can buy it locally, which is a plus.

Tip: A smoothie shaker bottle, also called a blender bottle, makes mixing much easier. If you're a smoothie fan, consider adding one of these to your kitchen for times you don't wish to (or can't) use the blender.

The amount of protein per serving in whey protein powders vary. The two I like are 16 and 22 grams, respectively. This amount is on the low end of the recommendations for an adult to have at each meal, based on daily needs. The recommended daily value (DV) of protein is 50 grams based on a 2,000 calorie a day diet. This is a rather arbitrary number.

A better way to figure your daily needs of protein is using a formula. The formula for the average sedentary adult is .8 grams of protein per kilogram of body weight (a kilogram is 2.20 pounds). Using an example from the Mayo Clinic, a person weighing 165 pounds needs 60 grams of protein per day.

Because we lose muscle mass as we age, this formula changes. After the age of 40, your needs may increase to 1 to 1.2 grams per kilogram, or 75 to 90 grams per day for the same body weight of 165 pounds. People who exercise regularly need between 1.1 and 1.7 grams per pound, depending on their level of exertion. Excessive protein is over 2 grams per kilogram of body weight—our 165-pound person would not want to exceed 150 grams, even if running ultramarathons.

Or maybe they would. Like almost everything, there are experts who do recommend elite athletes, and even those embarking on a new fitness routine, to meet or exceed that 2-gram level, topping out at 2.2 grams per kilogram. You may wish to keep this in mind if your physical activity suddenly increases.

Protein consumption should be spread throughout the day. Most people consume more protein in the evening than in the morning, but some studies show this is backward. Increasing protein in the morning may help you feel fuller throughout the day.

It's also important to note that protein intake should be calculated on lean body mass. If our 165-pound person has 20 percent body fat, their lean mass may only be 126 pounds (varies by height and gender). So you'd want to calculate your protein needs on the lean mass weight . . . or just go with the 50 grams a day and call it good.

Whey protein powder may or may not be something you should add to your food storage. Evaluate your needs and your food storage plan, along with your lifestyle and/or anticipated lifestyle.

Whey protein powder (along with collagen and gelatin discussed in the next section) make sense for my family based on the age of my husband and me (over 50) and our current lifestyle. We have a small homestead with daily chores, do martial arts, hike a few times a week, ski and snowshoe in the winter, and my husband is a runner. We use these supplements regularly.

The shelf life for these powders is only one or two years, depending on the brand and packaging. You may choose to leave it in the container it arrives in or repackage in vacuum-sealed containers. You'll want to practice the FIFO method and use whey protein powder in your daily life to make it realistic. Because of the cost, it's not something I'd want to put on a shelf and forget about until later. Later may mean past its expiration.

Collagen and Gelatin

While not the same, collagen and gelatin are similar enough to list together. Here's a helpful quote about the similarities:

"Collagen peptides are simply amino acids of gelatin broken down into smaller molecules through a natural process. The main difference between the two is that collagen is more therapeutic, and they also act a little differently in the kitchen. Gelatin gels when cooled after being mixed with liquids (think jiggly Jell-O) while collagen does not. Some of the studies cited here may use the simple term 'collagen' or use other names for it like 'hydrolyzed collagen' or 'collagen peptides.' These are all different names for the same thing." (From Trim Healthy Mama)

Collagen or gelatin mixed in warm water or tea can add much-needed protein. And both make a great addition to oatmeal, snack bars, protein bars, and more. I have a favorite breakfast, Creamy Rice, with both collagen and gelatin. This recipe was designed as a regular-cooked hot breakfast, but it's easily converted to a no-cook meal.

Quality collagen is around $1 per serving, with a single serving providing somewhere around 18 grams of protein (may vary slightly by brand). Gelatin from grass-raised beef is around 50¢ per serving, and Knox original unflavored gelatin (from what is likely factory raised pork) is in the neighborhood of 15¢ per serving. The amount of protein in each is in line with the cost—the higher cost has 6 to 12 grams of protein (based on brand), and the Knox has 2.

While gelatin doesn't pack the protein punch of collagen, its usefulness as a thickener may make up for that. Collagen is not a thickener and will not gel liquids.

Gelatin and collagen have a fairly long shelf life. While the recommendation for most brands is one year, I've used collagen that is more than five years old. The taste was fine, but I do wonder if the nutritional profile had changed.

Like whey protein powder, use this in your daily life to help it make sense as part of your food storage program. Stronger nails and shiny hair are a bonus of adding these to your diet! There's even some research showing collagen and gelatin can help you feel full and aid in weight loss while increasing brain function.

Cod Liver Oil

There's a whole host of supplements that could be discussed and considered for your no-cook food storage, things I've probably never even considered. But for the purpose of this book, I want to stick with more food-style supplements, and while cod liver oil isn't an actual food, the fat in it can help a person feel full while providing amazing nutritional benefits.

Dr. Weston A. Price discovered high doses of cod liver oil were a staple in many European societies. Cod liver oil is an excellent source of omega-3 fatty acids and contains decent amounts of Vitamins A and D. Dr. Price always combined cod liver oil with butter oil, which is still the recommendation from WAPF, to give maximum benefits. Butter oil is high in Vitamin K, which helps balance out the A and D in cod liver oil.

I like Green Pastures Cinnamon Tingle fermented cod liver oil/butter gel blend. I'll admit, the flavor takes some getting used to! I tried chocolate first, thinking that since I love chocolate, how can this not be good. *Wrong.*

You may need to try a few flavors and even brands before finding something that works for you. Some people prefer the gel capsules, but I found those kept "revisiting" me throughout the day. Cod liver oil burps are not something I'd recommend.

The supplement serving size of Green Pastures gel is ½ teaspoon, which gives 25 calories and 2.5 grams of fat. The cost per serving is around 50¢. This is another item I don't recommend storing and forgetting. There was some controversy a few years ago about rancidity in fermented cod liver oil. Bottom line, fish oil does expire. Usually, the best-by date gives around two years. After opening, it should be used within three to four months.

No-Cook Creamy Rice

During the winter months, we eat a lot of hot cereals. Leftover rice, with a few tasty and nourishing additions, makes a very filling breakfast. Leftover soaked brown rice is my favorite, but white, jasmine, and basmati are also tasty.

For our no-cook needs, I've adapted this recipe to use cold-soaked rice (you can find the original on my blog, Homespun Oasis). Put home-dehydrated, freeze-dried, or purchased instant rice in to soak before bed, and it'll be wonderfully creamy by morning. This recipe uses boiling water to provide a hot breakfast treat.

The original recipe is modified from a recipe in the *Trim Healthy Mama Cookbook*. It makes four average-size servings, with around 600 calories, 15 grams of protein (will vary based on brand of whey, collagen, and gelatin used), and 6 grams of fat. Most of the calories in this recipe are from the carbohydrates in the rice.

- 3 cups rice, cold soaked and fully hydrated
- ½ cup whey powder
- 4 cups boiling water, divided
- 1 teaspoon cinnamon or nutmeg (or both)
- ½ teaspoon powdered ginger
- ¼ cup collagen powder
- 1 tablespoon unflavored gelatin
- 1 teaspoon vanilla extract
- ½ teaspoon butter extract
- 1 to 2 pinches sea salt
- 2 small apples, diced; or 2 fresh bananas, sliced*
- 4 teaspoons coconut oil, MCT oil, butter, or ghee
- Your favorite sweetener, to taste

Put the rice in a large stockpot and top with the whey powder. Add extracts and fruit slices, then mix together.

In a separate bowl, combine spices, collagen, gelatin, and dry sweetener (if using liquid stevia, you'll add it in the next step). Combine to mix.

Measure out ½ cup of the boiling water. Set aside.

Add a small amount of the remaining boiling water to the collagen mixture, then stir with a fork or whisk to combine, trying to eliminate as many of the clumps that may occur as possible. Add a little more water, then stir again and add it to the rice.

Pour the remaining boiling water over the rice mixture (minus the ½ cup set aside). Stir to combine. Cover and let sit for a few minutes so everything warms through.

While the rice warms, add the coconut oil to the reserved ½ cup of boiling water, stirring to melt.

When the rice is warm and ready, divide into bowls. Top each bowl with ¼ of the water/coconut oil mixture. This mixture enhances the creamy quality, adding to the scrumptiousness. You can increase the creaminess with milk or cream as desired.

Add sweetener as desired to each bowl. Blackstrap molasses is a great one to consider for this recipe. It tastes wonderful and is an excellent source of iron, magnesium, potassium, calcium, and more. If using molasses, consider adding it when adding the hot water so it will melt into the rice.

*Substitute dehydrated fruit for fresh in this recipe. Apples, berries, and raisins are all wonderful. Rehydrate by putting in water the night before. You want about 1 to 1½ cups of rehydrated fruit. Frozen and defrosted apples also work, as do frozen berries or even canned fruit. If using frozen or canned fruit, add when assembling the cereal.

Ready-Made Meals and Snacks

Commercial snack foods, such as granola bars, breakfast bars, and crackers, are great ready-to-eat items. But these have a higher cost per ounce than many other options, and the shelf life is limited.

While we do keep these on hand, they're a part of our everyday foods—quick snacks to grab on the way out the door—as opposed to food storage items. Like most things, some snack foods are better than others. Check the ingredients and choose items you are comfortable with.

I used to try and keep store-bought jerky on hand to use in our get-home bags, or 72-hour kits. Since we keep our homemade jerky in the freezer, I wanted something with a room temperature shelf life. Sadly, this jerky has a problem of walking off in my house!

Now we limit this store-bought jerky to purchasing as needed. It's a treat more than anything and is something we look forward to taking on hikes or backpacking adventures. Your results with this jerky may be different, and it may be a good addition to your no-cook food storage.

MREs

You may also wish to consider Meals Ready to Eat (MREs). Although not truly a no-cook option since they contain a heating pack, many people like the convenience of having an entire meal in one container, including sides and a beverage. Plus, they are fully shelf stable.

When we first started our preparedness journey, MREs weren't widely available. I'd heard rumors of buying them at Army surplus stores, and even visited one and asked about them, but I never actually found any. Now a quick google search shows them on just about every major retail site. Are they real MREs?

I've found conflicting information as to whether the "US Military surplus" MREs being widely sold are genuine or not. Some sources say yes, that they're MREs the military has expired and someone bought in lots to resell. Others say buyers beware. Of course, some of those most critical about military surplus MREs being sold to civilians are those with skin in the game—manufacturers of civilian MREs!

At $10 to $15+ per meal, they're not something we've chosen to add to our food storage. You may come to a different decision. I've included a few articles and information in the Resources section to help you research MREs to see if they may be right for your no-cook food storage.

Even though MREs aren't right for us at this time, we do have a small supply of self-heating meals. My husband found a great deal on these at a local scratch-and-dent store. He bought three to try and liked them enough he returned for a couple dozen more to use during hunting season.

Unlike military MREs, which are complete meals and contain around 1,250 calories and one-third the recommended dietary allowance (RDA) of vitamins and minerals, these are only around 300 calories and about a tenth of the RDA for select items—except sodium. Like most processed foods, they tend to be high in sodium. I'll admit, I haven't eaten these but was there when my husband did his test on them. He sampled a few different flavors, declaring the spaghetti and meatballs as not bad.

The convenience of the heating element will be good for hunting trips and perfect for power outages. But if you're looking for no-odor foods, it may not be a good fit. When he opened it up, it truly did fill the house with the aroma of spaghetti.

Ration Bars

You're probably familiar with emergency food bars, or ration bars. These densely packaged bars taste a little like pie crust. They are usually available in 1,200, 2,400, or 3,600 calories. Those with 2,400 and 3,600 calories are designed to be broken into pieces to give you 1,200 calories a day. While they may keep you from starving, they're nothing to write home about!

I'm not a fan of pie crust, and these are especially dry and crumbly, needing to be washed down with plenty of water. But with a five-year shelf life, and opening the package being the only preparation needed, they do have a use. We keep one in each backpack when going out on multiday hikes. If we were to get lost or separated, we'd have this in addition to our regular pack food.

Ration bars are somewhere between $5 and $10 each, depending on the brand and calorie count. The pie crust consistency is often dressed up with cinnamon or lemon flavoring. I recommend buying a few different varieties to taste before ordering a specific brand in bulk. Some are better than others.

Similar to ration bars, yet different, are backpacking meal bars. These are less of a ration bar—without the pie crust flavor—and more like a granola or cereal bar but higher in calories. Where granola bars and other snack bars have 100 to 200 calories, these backpacking meal bars are around 650 calories. There may be several brands of these, but the one I'm familiar with is vegan and not bad tasting. The ingredients are also better than expected.

Runner's Gel

This is something new we have around our place. My husband has long loved jogging, and recently, he's taken to longer runs and entering races.

Runner's gel, or energy gel, is used by long-distance runners to replenish glycogen stores.

Glycogen is the stored form of glucose in our bodies. Running burns glycogen. Each of us stores approximately 1½ to 2 hours of glycogen, but fast runners can deplete this well before that time. Running beyond glycogen stores can cause light-headedness, lead legs, and brain fog. Some people refer to this as bonking.

While this is often spoken about among long-distance runners, bicyclists and hikers can also bonk. Anytime you expend energy beyond your glycogen stores, you could bonk. Frequent snacks help, especially those with concentrated sugars and/or salt. There're many whole foods or less-processed options for this, such as dried fruit, applesauce pouches, pretzels, honey straws, mashed potato pouches, and more. But the easy solution, and one used by many distance runners, is energy gels.

Energy gels are not only a quick source of simple sugars, but many also contain electrolytes—needed for salty sweaters—and/or caffeine, which can give an extra energy boost.

My husband's been experimenting with a few different types of gels to find what works for him. His max runs right now are only about 2½ hours in length, so he doesn't need much for his glycogen boost. He does carry three different pouches with him, in a pocket on his hydration backpack, when he's doing anything farther than a 5K so he has them if he begins to bonk.

Because these are now part of our lifestyle, we've added a small assortment to our pantry. While the primary purpose is for my husband's runs, they're also added to our packs for longer hikes, and we have them in case of emergency. If we didn't have these specific uses for them, I doubt we'd consider storing them.

Keep in mind, using all your glycogen stores is possible anytime you are working your body and expending energy. Cutting wood, digging, manually harvesting a hay or similar field, walking a long distance . . . all of these expend energy. Plan on needing a glycogen boost and replacing electrolytes.

Energy gels have somewhere around 100 calories per packet, with most of it being from carbohydrates (sugar). They provide simple and immediate energy and little more. The cost is 75¢ to $1.50 per packet. The best-by date on our gels ranges from about six months to a year. Because of the way they're packaged, and with cool and dark storage, I suspect they'll be fine well beyond this date. I'm sure it is obvious, but I'll say it anyway: energy gels are not WAPF recommended.

Electrolyte Drinks

During the summers, my husband has a very physically demanding job where he digs a lot of holes. He uses a homemade electrolyte replacement of water, sea salt, apple cider vinegar, and stevia. When he runs a race, I also bring along a shaker of sea salt in case he needs an extra sodium boost at the end. We add it to his water.

There're many commercial electrolyte drinks—either liquid or powders to add to water. I'll admit to not knowing much about these, since we have always made our own. The addition of magnesium and potassium to these homemade mixes is also a good idea. Check the Resources section for links to recipes.

I do think it's a good idea to research and have a few recipes and/or store these items. Likely, the powders have a longer shelf life than the liquid. These drinks are not only good for hot work in the sun when electrolyte stores can be depleted, but also for illness. Diarrhea can be deadly for babies, children, elderly, or any compromised individual.

Bean Roll-Ups

I debated whether to add this recipe. On one hand, it's a standby for when we do long hikes or backpacking trips. On the other hand, for those times, we use easy-to-purchase and widely available store-bought flour tortillas as the main component for the roll-up.

While it certainly meets the criteria of no-cook, it's not really a true food storage option. I've decided it's too good to leave out! I've written this recipe as we eat it now, but I'll also offer suggestions to make this work with only food storage items as no-cook or low-cook meals.

The original idea for this roll-up is from *The Hungry Spork: A Long Distance Hiker's Guide to Meal Planning* by Inga Aksamit. In her book, she describes how a bandanna becomes her plate for assembling this easy lunch. That's how we do it now too! Just set out the bandanna, put the tortilla on it, then load it up. Easy and delicious!

This is a great use of home-dehydrated beans and rice, as well as waxed Parmesan cheese. Commercially freeze-dried black bean burger in the #10 can also makes a great filling, along with commercially purchased instant rice.

You could make tortillas, crepes, or even pancakes (see the Chapter on Fuel-Saving and Low-Odor Cooking Methods for tips). You can also try the filling in nori, rice paper, or lettuce leaves. Or forget the roll-up and pile the filling on crackers from your food storage, or just eat it with a fork. These are instructions for filling one roll-up. Scale up as needed.

- ¼ to ⅓ cup dehydrated or freeze-dried bean mash
- ¼ to ⅓ cup dehydrated rice or instant rice
- Spices (see notes)
- Parmesan cheese, shredded or sliced (or cheese of choice)
- Sunflower, pumpkin, or chia seeds, or freeze-dried corn
- Jerky or jerky-style bites (see notes)

An hour or longer before you're ready to eat, combine the bean mash and rice in a container. Add ½ to ⅔ cup of water, depending on how much mash and rice you start with; you want an equal amount of water. Stir to combine. Add your spices of choice. Let rehydrate.

When ready to eat, lay out your tortilla (or alternative) and spread the bean and rice mixture over the top. Top with cheese and a heavy sprinkle of seeds or corn to give some crunch. Then slice or tear the jerky and add it. Roll up and enjoy.

Notes:

You can choose the spices for this. I tend to try and match my spice to my bean choice. I use Mexican spices, like chili powder and cumin, for pinto or black beans. Curry powder or paprika go great with lentils. Salt and pepper to taste. When using the freeze-dried bean burger, I find it needs nothing further.

Thick and soft commercially purchased jerky or jerky bites are great with this, but home-processed jerky strips are sometimes a little tough. You can cut them and add to the beans and rice when soaking to help soften them. Home-processed jerky made from ground meat works well, either using the soaking method or cutting and adding at the end.

You could also consider using tuna or salmon from pouches or make it without any meat. The combination of rice and beans makes a complete protein.

Raw Protein

How could I create a no-cook cookbook without at least discussing raw protein as an option? It's true that raw meat won't be part of your pantry, but many of us do keep meat "on the hoof," or live in an area where there's considerably fewer humans than wildlife and *may* have some hunting and/or fishing opportunities.

I've long been a fan of sushi and sashimi. When I first heard of steak tartare, I thought it sounded interesting but wasn't sure I really wanted to eat my beef fully raw. Rare to medium-rare steak, yum. But raw . . . hmm.

My first opportunity to try raw beef wasn't tartare but rather carpaccio—the Italian version as opposed to French tartare. My first bite was with a little trepidation, but after that . . . mercy! It was amazing.

So amazing that, when I got home, I grabbed my *Nourishing Traditions* book and quickly turned to the carpaccio recipe. For several months, I made and remade it, tweaking and changing it. It was so good! I also tried a few of the other raw meat recipes in the book, reworking those to fit my family too.

If raw protein may be an option for you, explore it now so you have a recipe, or ten, to rely on. Make sure you have the needed condiments and seasonings to make the raw meat or fish the best it can be.

Also know that raw meat or fish is always a risk. Truly, most food probably carries some risk with it. But when prepared properly, along with safe handling practices, the risk of foodborne illness is reduced. Use fresh, high-quality meat or fish. Clean utensils and hands (consider handling with gloves), being mindful of temperatures. Ideally, the meat or fish should be refrigerated at all times, except during actual preparation and serving.

Steak tartare, carpaccio, and sashimi are just a few of the worldwide raw meat dishes. Plus, there are many marinated, salted, or acid "cooked" dishes, which may also fall under this raw protein category. Recently, I started hearing about chicken sashimi. This is where I draw the line on raw meat.

Chicken sashimi, sometimes called chicken tartare, is often prepared by boiling or searing chicken for only ten seconds. Ten seconds! What's that going to do? Chicken not only carries the risk of salmonella but also campylobacter, a bacteria found in their intestines.

Some trendy restaurants around the world, including in the US, serve this raw chicken. Most do try and source from local farmers to give the highest-quality product available.

As someone who raises chickens and watches how they walk around the farm and the things they'll peck at, I'll stick with enjoying my chicken fully cooked, thank you very much. Boiling, braising, or steaming chicken are perfect fuel-saving and low-odor cooking methods. We'll discuss these options more in the next chapter.

Fuel-Saving and Low-Odor Cooking Methods

My goal is to give you as many tools in your food storage arsenal as possible. So, it seems the perfect way to finish this book that details no-cook food storage is by offering ideas on how to cook while saving fuel and/or reducing cooking odors.

Saving Fuel When Using Your Range

If you're keeping the electric, natural gas, or propane bill down during a time of unemployment, underemployment, or tight budgeting, these tips will help.

- Use shallow, wide pots that cover the heating elements or flame as much as possible and/or use a smaller burner.
- Put a lid on your pot to hold in the heat.
- Don't heat longer than needed. If it only needs to be warm, don't boil it.
- Use a kitchen timer or other reminder so you don't forget you have something heating.
- Use a whistling teakettle when boiling water. The whistle will let you know it's ready; otherwise, you may forget you have water heating in a pan.
- Move hot water or coffee to a thermos to keep warm for later.
- When cooking pasta, rice, and other grains, use the bare minimum amount of water. Experiment with what amount works best.
- Soaking or sprouting foods before cooking will drastically reduce cooking times.
- Many items, like pasta and some whole grains, can be brought to a boil, then covered and the heat turned off. They will continue to cook and soften in the hot water.
- Cook once, eat multiple times. Example: cook a large pot of beans, take out what you need for today's meal, and spice as desired. The rest can be reheated for later, using less fuel than

cooking dry beans. Learn more about this in my book *Stretchy Beans*. Use the same concept for rice, oatmeal, and other grains.

- Use a pressure cooker. Many items, like beans, can be cooked in a pressure cooker in only minutes instead of hours. If you've soaked and/or sprouted the beans first, this time is reduced even further.

- When using the oven, cook more than one item at a time—bread alongside a casserole, a cake alongside a roast.

- Does the oven really need to be preheated? Casseroles and roasts can go into cold ovens. Some bread recipes start in a cold oven. When cooking multiple items at one time, start with the items that can go in a cold oven and then, after it's heated, add your other dishes.

Alternative Cooking Methods

During the 2007 Great Coastal Gale, our power was out for six days. Our all-electric house was nearly unusable, especially the kitchen. We did our cooking on a single-burner propane stove, even heating water for dishes on it. Early in our preparedness journey, we knew we wanted more alternative cooking methods.

When we first moved to Wyoming in 2009, our home was on liquefied petroleum gas (LPG), or simply referred to as propane. When the power would go out, which it did on a regular basis, the stovetop still worked when lit with a match. The match was needed because the igniter didn't work without electricity. The oven was also out of commission without electricity, without a simple workaround like lighting a match to start the pilot.

Having the stovetop is a huge help when the power is out, but we knew we wanted something more when building our homestead. The range we have now is an off-grid propane range. It doesn't connect to the house electric but does have batteries (eight AAs) that spark the igniter. No worries at all if the power goes out, as long as the batteries are still good. If the batteries go bad and we can't replace them, the stovetop will still light manually with a match and, even better, the oven works.

Most modern gas or propane ovens have a safety feature that prevent them from being manually lit in a power outage. But our off-grid range doesn't have this feature, making it fully usable without the batteries.

There're several brands of off-grid ranges on the market now. Some may have different features than others, use different size batteries, etc. You'll want to do your research to ensure you get what you need for your specific lifestyle. They do tend to cost several hundred dollars more than their non-off-grid counterparts.

In addition to our off-grid range, we have several other alternative cooking methods.

Instant Pot: On a sunny day, my small- to medium-sized solar system powers this perfectly. A generator may also run an Instant Pot, but please consider the noise of the generator. If you're trying to be stealth, a loud generator isn't very covert. Solar generators are quiet but provide varying amounts of power. If you're considering a solar generator, price it out and compare with a small solar system. You may be surprised at what your money can—or can't—get.

Woodstove: We only heat our house with wood. From about the end of October to the end of March, the fire is rarely out. The flat top has a special grate to allow for cooking. Before our kitchen was finished and our off-grid range was installed, we made almost everything on the top of the woodstove.

I've even experimented with baking inside the woodstove, using it as an oven. My tip for this is to make sure the fire is barely going or burning out; otherwise, it's much too hot. If you plan it correctly, you can bake bread inside the firebox (in a Dutch oven). Potatoes, turnips, and even a small roast are also worth trying inside a woodstove with the fire nearly burned out.

Propane stoves: These small camping stoves are safe to use indoors, with proper precautions. You need adequate space and ventilation, while limiting their use. When building our house, we used a two-burner stove in our kitchen, but only for items with a short cooking time. Essentially, things that only needed a quick heat up.

Be sure to combine the fuel-saving tips listed above to cut down on propane use. We only use the small one-pound propane containers inside and ensure it is turned off after use. The larger containers are only safe for outdoor use. We also have a carbon monoxide detector on each level of our home. A butane stove is another option.

There're several options for outdoor cooking. Here are a few of my favorites:

- Rocket stove (these use small diameters of wood; we even use sagebrush)
- Sun Oven (big cost upfront, but uses only the power of the sun)
- Propane grill
- Backpacker's stove (there are a variety of options with several fuel choices)
- Charcoal or wood grill
- Fire pit with a grate
- Bean hole or pit cooking

For conserving fuel, the Sun Oven is amazing. We use ours for stews, soups, and even making breads and desserts. It does take some monitoring to follow the sun. The large reflectors also catch the wind, making it impractical on windy Wyoming days. The cost of the Sun Oven is high, but there are other brands of solar cookers you may wish to explore.

Low-Odor Cooking

When focusing on low-odor cooking, you want to avoid cooking methods that release abundant aromas, while also avoiding strong-smelling foods. Think about the smell of frying bacon and how well it travels. Frying, baking, roasting, grilling, and even toasting are all high-odor cooking methods.

Many of the fuel-saving ideas, especially those for indoor use, can double for low-odor. In an urban area, you'll want to evaluate how odors usually carry. I lived in an apartment complex where the downstairs and next-door neighbor's food smells were super strong. If you experience this now, you'll certainly have it in an emergency situation. And hungry people may show up at your door. You may want to use the super guerrilla no-cook tactics during the height of the emergency.

When is the height of an emergency? The common advice has always leaned toward the first three days of a severe situation being a grace period of sorts. The belief is, since most people keep only three days' worth of food on hand, things will fall apart on day four. You could use those first three days to cook up and preserve as much fresh or frozen food as possible by canning, dehydrating, fermenting, salting, or other methods.

You may have more freedom for indoor cooking in a suburban or rural area. But keep in mind, food odors do travel. Even in my rural area of 20- to 40-plus-acre lots, we know when someone is barbecuing!

Woodstoves are great for heat and cooking, but the smoke escaping the chimney is a dead giveaway that a home is occupied. If you're going super stealth, you may wish to only have fires after dark. The smoke smell will still travel, but it may be more difficult to find its location in the dark of night than in the light of day.

It's difficult to contain odors using outdoor cooking methods. The exception is the Sun Oven. Keeping the door shut holds in the aromas. I've cooked in the Sun Oven and carefully folded up the panels and carried it in the house before opening as a test. This works well and really helps with the odors.

If you must cook outside, consider cooking after dark or very early in the morning when most people are sleeping. Little to no wind is also helpful to keep the food smells from traveling.

Boiling

Boiling is a low-odor cooking method. To conserve fuel when cooking something that needs a long boil, you can bring it to a full boil and then, after it's good and hot, move it to a nonelectric slow cooker, haybox cooker, or a pseudo haybox made from an old cooler and some towels. This works great! You still need to use your stovetop, woodstove, or other burner to start the process, but the cooking time is limited.

A thermos can also work as a haybox, on a smaller scale. This is ideal for things like pasta. Put the pasta in the bottom, add boiling water, and let it sit. Cooking times vary from minutes to hours, depending on what you're cooking. Be sure to use enough water so it can properly absorb. This is a great way to heat up sprouted lentils, sprouted garbanzo beans, oatmeal, and more.

It's also perfect for rehydrating dehydrated or freeze-dried foods. I would not recommend attempting to cook shrimp in your thermos. I tried that once . . . the smell was terrible. I ended up throwing my nice thermos in the garbage.

Some foods don't even need the insulation of the haybox or thermos. A good boil and time are enough. Try this with pasta, oatmeal, sprouted lentils, or sprouted garbanzos. Hard beans, like pintos, do better with the insulation.

Since boiling water is odor free, you can also heat up those soaked pastas from the Noodles and Flakes chapter. After they've soaked and are nearly soft (slightly less than al dente), carefully add them to a pot of salted boiling water. Give it a stir, turn off the heat, and let it sit for one to two minutes. Taste for doneness and allow to sit longer if needed.

Poaching is also low odor. Even fish can be poached with little residual aroma. Sous vide is another low-odor cooking method worth exploring. While this isn't something I do at home, one of my neighbors loves her sous vide setup. This method is a little like poaching, in that you use water, but the meat is put in a vacuum-sealed bag before submersing.

While vacuum sealing may not be realistic, especially in a power-out situation, there are some foods you can sous vide using a zipper bag. Making sure as much air is removed as possible is imperative for sous vide and the challenge with zipper bags. That and you can't do something that needs to cook for an extended time. Of course, since you'll be conserving fuel, that won't be an issue.

Steaming and Simmering

My friend Wardee from Traditional Cooking School opened my eyes to the wonders of an Instant Pot. One of her most convincing articles for why I needed to add one to my off-grid home was the way she used it for leftovers. Being a microwave-free home (while off-grid, before going off-grid, and even now), I love tricks for heating leftovers. Wardee's trick: she steamed them in the Instant Pot! It's not only brilliant but really works.

Steaming is something to consider for your low-odor cooking. There are many, many foods that steam well, such as chicken cut into small pieces, vegetables, and seafood. Have you ever had dim sum? Many of these are steamed.

Small bites of meats, rice, dumplings, noodles, spring rolls, buns, and more are all candidates for steaming. There's likely to still be some odor from the food itself, but by limiting your spices, you may help combat that.

Steaming vegetables or eggs is perfect in a folding steamer basket. Dim sum is usually done in traditional layered bamboo steamers. There's also a variety of stainless-steel stacking steamers.

Simmering with a lid on will also help hold in odors. To simmer, you want the water just below boiling. Tough cuts of meat respond well to a long, slow simmer. Bones that might be thrown away can be simmered into a nourishing stock or broth. The woodstove is my preferred device for long simmers since I'm already using that fuel.

Miscellaneous Methods and Ideas

Fish and meats cooked in parchment paper—en papillote—tend to hold in aromas fairly well during the cooking time. I've done trout in parchment on a wood or charcoal grill many times. Other than the smell of the smoke, there was no food odor. Try this method with beef, wild game, or pork, and tuck in vegetables for a complete meal. Experiment with it now so you have trusted recipes and know it'll limit aromas if needed.

A dry skillet may be an option for lowish-odor cooking and baking. Tortillas, flatbreads, crepes, and pancakes will still produce some aroma, but when cooking inside with the windows closed, the smells should be low enough to contain them if you aren't in a super densely populated area.

If you must roast, consider using a pit (at night) or you could try oven bags and a roasting pan, which may help contain the aromas. Aluminum foil may also be something to try.

Think about the herbs and spices you use. I'm a huge fan of curry, but it has a very distinctive and pungent aroma. Using curry inside may work, but outside might carry too far.

Try a charcoal splatter screen. A splatter screen is a great way to keep your cooktop clean. Taking it a step further, the charcoal version will also cut down on odors, as the charcoal absorbs them during cooking.

Keep things clean. Not only do you need to think about odors while cooking, but also afterward. Have a plan for your trash and garbage to avoid that stink and to keep people from seeing what you have, in addition to smelling it. Keeping things clean will not only help with unwanted human visitors, but animals too.

Simple Bean Dip

This is a delicious and simple bean dip, spread, or sauce and is perfect with veggies, crackers, or flatbread wedges. Find sourdough recipes in my book *Sourdough for Your Food Storage*.

This simple bean dip was originally shared in *Sprouts for Your Food Storage*. While I normally cook hard beans before eating, this recipe uses raw sprouted beans. If you prefer to cook your beans first, a light steaming is all they need.

Remember! Kidney beans are not safe to eat raw and are not suitable for this recipe.

- 1 cup sprouted pinto, chickpea, white, or black beans (or a combination if that's how you roll)
- ¼ cup water
- ¼ teaspoon sea salt
- Scant ¼ teaspoon garlic powder

- 1 to 2 dashes ground black pepper
- ¼ teaspoon ground cumin
- 1 tablespoon nutritional yeast or Parmesan cheese (the kind from a can is fine)
- 1 teaspoon lemon juice
- 1 tablespoon extra-virgin olive oil

Combine all ingredients in a food processor (electric or manual). Depending on the size of your processor, you may need to do this in batches. Process until mixed. Check for consistency. You may need to add a little water, 1 tablespoon at a time. You can keep processing until fully smooth or leave it a little chunky; the choice is yours!

Tip: If you end up with a thinner dip than you wish, stir in a little extra nutritional yeast or Parmesan cheese to thicken. Add additional seasonings after processing to adjust the flavors.

This can be served cold (best with chickpeas, think hummus) or warm (fabulous when using pinto or black beans). If serving warm, you can add shredded cheddar cheese and a dash or two of your favorite hot sauce. Either way is yummy.

Simple Bean Dip also works as an easy sauce with just a few tweaks. To 1 cup cold bean dip (any variety), add 2 teaspoons Dijon mustard and 2 teaspoons Sucanat (or Rapadura or maple syrup). Whisk together until smooth.

Now evaluate your sauce. It probably needs to be thinner. Add water, 1 tablespoon at a time, until you reach your desired consistency. Try this sauce on fresh greens or steamed vegetables.

Complete-Protein Sprouted Bread

This is a variation on my Two-Ingredient Sprouted Bread found in *Sprouts for Your Food Storage*. That recipe is made with only sprouted wheat and salt. This one uses a variety of sprouted grains and beans (think Ezekiel bread) to turn your bread into a complete protein. The combination of beans and grains gives all nine amino acids needed for a complete protein.

This is fabulous cooked in the crockpot, resulting in a super-moist bread. A Sun Oven is also a great cooking device for a moist loaf. If cooking on top of a woodstove, it is best with something like a double boiler set up so the bread can steam rather than bake. For regular oven baking, add a dish of water to help steam the loaf. As written, this makes a small loaf. Scale up as needed.

- ½ cup sprouted wheat, barley, spelt, einkorn, or other large grain
- ½ cup sprouted beans (lentils are traditional, but any can be used except kidney beans)

178

- ¼ cup sprouted millet or quinoa
- ½ teaspoon sea salt

Mix all ingredients in a food processor. If using a manual food processor, you may need to process in batches. Pulse until it's chopped enough to stick together so you can form your loaf. Then pulse a little more. I like it to be a somewhat smooth dough with a few larger pieces, but you may prefer something a little chunkier.

Note: If it isn't pulsed enough, it will crumble after baking. You may wish to pulse to very smooth the first time and adjust on future batches.

If using a crockpot, shape to fit, then cook on low for 8 hours.

If using a Sun Oven, shape to fit your pan. Bake at low heat with the lid on, around 225°, until cooked through. Leave the lid closed on the oven so it will collect condensation and help steam the bread. This may take several hours.

If using an oven, lightly grease a cookie sheet. Shape into a round, baguette, rolls, breadsticks, etc. Bake in a low-heat oven, around 225°, until cooked through, maybe somewhere around an hour. This will vary depending on your loaf. Small loaves (buns) will cook quicker.

To cook on top of the woodstove, use a lidded Dutch oven or spider (the kind of Dutch oven with the little legs). Put your loaf in another container that will fit inside the oven. I use a round 8" cake pan. Add a small amount of water, not enough to go into the cake pan but to steam while it bakes. Check the water frequently while baking. How long? This will depend on how hot your fire is and how large your loaf is.

Resources

Check out the Resources page that goes along with this book for more recipes, information, and helpful tools: HomespunOasis.com/No-Cook-Resources.

Find more information on traditional cooking, preparedness, and homesteading on my website: HomespunOasis.com

Sources

(Source 1) Legumes and Pulse Harvard T.H. Chan School of Public Health:
https://www.hsph.harvard.edu/nutritionsource/legumes-pulses/

(Source 2) *Nourishing Traditions: The Cookbook that Challenges Politically Correct Nutrition and the Diet Dictocrats* Revised Second Edition by Sally Fallon with Mary G. Enig, PhD

(Source 3) "Great Recession, Great Recovery? Trends from the Current Population Survey":
https://www.bls.gov/opub/mlr/2018/article/great-recession-great-recovery.htm

(Source 4) "Frequent Canned Food Use is Positively Associated with Nutrient-Dense Food Group Consumption and Higher Nutrient Intakes in US Children and Adults":
https://www.ncbi.nlm.nih.gov/pmc/articles/PMC4517017/

(Source 5) "Potassium Iodide Tablet Alternatives":
https://www.doomandbloom.net/potassium-iodide-alternatives/

(Source 6) "Is it Safe to Make Flavored Oils with Garlic or Fresh Vegetables?":
https://ask.usda.gov/s/article/Is-it-safe-to-make-flavored-oils-with-garlic-or-fresh-vegetables

Also by Millie Copper

Sourdough for Your Food Storage: Add Nutrition and Variety to Your Baked Goods

Want to make tasty treats your whole family will love? Are you looking for a great way to expand your food storage grains?

Sourdough For Your Food Storage will show you how! Not only will you learn how to make delicious, crusty breads, but also biscuits, main dishes, and even desserts! Sourdough is a healthier alternative to yeast, and it tastes great to boot.

Sprouts for Your Food Storage: Add Nutrition and Variety to Your Diet

Want to make delicious, healthy sprouts that your whole family will love?

Sprouts for Your Food Storage will show you how! Sprouts are an easy, cheap, and tasty vegetable anyone can grow. They require little space and can be done without any special equipment. Because the original product grows during the sprouting process, this is a great way to stretch a small amount into a larger amount.

Real Food Hits the Road: Budget-Friendly Tips, Ideas, and Recipes for Enjoying Real Food Away from Home

Are you planning to hit the road for a family vacation? Do you want to take a road trip, but the idea of eating out three meals a day doesn't work for your budget or your health?

Real Food Hits the Road will be your guide to saving the budget, keeping your digestion working well, and eating real food away from home while letting you enjoy the trip and not "cook" all of the time.

Stock the Real Food Pantry: Save Money and Time While Gaining Peace of Mind

Do you want to stock your pantry with nutritious food your family will actually eat? In these trying times, are you focusing on your food storage?

If so, *Stock the Real Food Pantry* has you covered. Learn how a wonderfully stocked real food pantry will save you money and time— while giving you peace of mind.

Design a Dish: Save Your Food Dollars!

Would you like to learn great methods to reduce food waste? What if you could enjoy one meal for "free" each week?

Design a Dish will teach you how to make wonderful, simple dishes you can prepare day in and day out. You'll be amazed at how easy it is to nourish your family with these tasty dishes!

Stretchy Beans: Nutritious, Economical Meals the Easy Ways

Do you struggle with feeding your family delicious, healthy meals? Are you tired of trying to figure out what's for dinner each night? Do you cringe when you see how much money your family spends on groceries each month?

If so, *Stretchy Beans* is the solution you've been looking for! Learn how to easily prepare dinners that the whole family will love—while staying on budget, spending less time in the kitchen, and not losing your sanity.

About the Author

Millie Copper, writer of Cozy Apocalyptic Fiction and preparedness mentor, was born in Nebraska but never lived there. Her parents fully embraced wanderlust and moved regularly, giving her an advantage of being from nowhere and everywhere.

Millie Copper lives in the wilds of Wyoming with her husband and young son, tending chickens and attempting a food forest on their small homestead. After living off the grid for several years, they've recently gone back on the grid. Four adult daughters, three sons-in-law, four grandchildren, and one more on the way round out the family.

Since 2009, Millie has authored articles on traditional foods, alternative health, homesteading, and preparedness-many times all within the same piece. Millie has penned seven nonfiction, traditional food focused books, sharing how, with a little creativity, anyone can transition to a real foods diet without overwhelming their food budget.

The twelve-installment *Havoc in Wyoming* Christian Post-Apocalyptic fiction series uses her homesteading, off-the-grid, and preparedness lifestyle as a guide. The adventure continues with the newly released *Montana Mayhem* series.

Find Millie at www.MillieCopper.com
Facebook: www.facebook.com/MillieCopperAuthor/
Amazon: www.amazon.com/author/MillieCopper
BookBub: https://www.bookbub.com/authors/Millie-Copper

www.ingramcontent.com/pod-product-compliance
Lightning Source LLC
Chambersburg PA
CBHW061157120626
46546CB00005B/2093